# THROUGH THE LONELINESS

## *A Woman's Spiritual Journal*

Antonia J. van den Beld

Paulist Press
New York/Mahwah

Book design by Celine M. Allen

Cover and interior art by William Hart McNichols

Library of Congress Cataloging-in-Publication Data

van den Beld, Antonia, 1935–
    Through the loneliness.

    1. Van den Beld, Antonia, 1935–    . Diaries.
2. Catholics—United States—Biography. 3. Middle aged women—
Religious life.    I. Title
BX4705.V3125A3    1987        248.8'43        87–13683
ISBN 0-8091-2913-2

Published by Paulist Press
997 Macarthur Boulevard
Mahwah, New Jersey 07430

Printed and bound in the
United States of America

# Introduction

This journal movingly records the human and spiritual features of a "second" journey thrust upon a woman in her middle years. The crisis of feelings is there—in her anger, fear, guilt and, above all, the emotions stirred up by relationships. The image of a journey (the "road of no return") weaves in and out of the story. The writer constantly questions herself about sin, personal responsibility and the values which might guide her traveling. She suffers from loneliness as she feels her life taken in new directions. One or two companions show up. The final days of the journal may be signaling journey's end in the longing for a simplicity which still leaves her ready to share in the life of the institutional Church.

I was grateful to find toward the close of the story that my own *The Second Journey* (Paulist Press, 1978) had helped the writer to confront her experience and guide her response. Piecing together various clues (including the moving account of her dream), I concluded that there was a terrifying depth of suffering below the gentle movement of the author's journal.

God, God's grace and the drama of our human possibilities for love form the centerpiece of this story. The entry for September 10, 1980 brilliantly defines that ultimate challenge: Are we capable of truly caring for other people? The early weeks of 1983 show the writer trying to persuade herself that love is not by its very nature reciprocal, still wrestling with the harsh difficulty of detachment in love, and then finally reconciled to the mysterious life coming from that divine love which we can never earn and never deserve.

The literature of midlife journeys will be richer with the publication of this journal. We readers will view the story from a cool distance. But it was a pilgrimage painful to live through and perhaps even more painful to record.

Gerald O'Collins, S.J.

The Gregorian University
Rome, 4 August 1986

To Thomas,
who had to see
with his own eyes.

*I awakened you under the apple tree,*
*there where your mother conceived you,*
*there where she who gave birth to you conceived you.*
*Song of Songs 8:5*

*January 9, 1980*      Why, for heaven's sake, did God complicate people's life
the way it seems to have been done?
Plants are plants,
animals are animals,
but people are not just people.
A human being does not have only his human nature to
contend with.
Man has a glimpse of something Other.
He has seen a glimmer of Truth somewhere beyond.
He has been promised heaven—and he is left to die on earth.
We are confronted with a life in us utterly unlike us.
We are faced with the reality that we can be "touched,"
that we can "respond,"
and that, when we do, we live a life which is not our own.
And then, as I said, we are left to die on earth.
We have no other way,
no other outlet,
no other means than our human nature. . . .
Do we?
Yet we are asked to walk on water.

What does it mean to believe in God's grace?
I mean, it doesn't work like magic, does it?
From the way God "lifts us up" only "to let us down,"
it looks as though we are expected to get in on the act.

How?


*January 10*      How can it be that I experience myself as a religious person
and at the same time have such little faith?
    I am "playing my little game with religion," the kids tell
me.

*January 11*

Why these notes? I am writing in the hopes of sorting out myself. It is so easy to reason-around full circle and end up where you started out. Maybe keeping up, on paper, helps me see where I am coming from. I say I haven't given up my faith, but in fact I am not traveling the road I set out on—and I don't know where I am heading.

Yesterday was a bad day—same old story: I can't sort out my "feelings." I don't know how to get in or out of them—or around them. "It isn't really beyond you to suffer through them," some inner voice whispered into my ear. My son told me differently: "You are in a bad mood!" In fact, I haven't been in a visibly bad mood for a long time—and come to think of it, it wasn't as bad as it could have been. Anyway, feelings are confusing and misleading and lead to self-centeredness. I have to get away from them. There must be a way of judging the affairs of the heart or the spirit, other than through feelings. But how?

✳

From a Day of Recollection:
We are vulnerable.
If we want to appear invulnerable,
we create tension within ourselves.
We feel "untruthful."
We—hate ourselves. . . .

*January 13*

It was six-thirty this morning when one of the kids walked into the bedroom and asked sweetly:
"Do you have a nice picture of Jesus on the cross?"
I searched my doubtful mind and answered, "No."
Later at breakfast: "Too bad you don't have a picture!"
"What do you need it for?" I ventured to ask.

4

"Oh, we have to bring a picture to the art history class of our ideal man—as nude as possible—and Jesus would just freak them out—but never mind, I have a picture of Mick Jagger!"

*January 17*

It is what I call the times-in-between that are hard—the times that I feel removed—out of touch. It is this feeling of unrelatedness that I am fighting; wondering all the time where it comes from. Did I bring it on myself? I conclude that must be so—so I must find a way back—I think—but how? How . . . if I am out of touch?

Does whatever happens to me happen with the knowledge and the foresight and the consent (?) of God? How much does He run our lives? Think of Jonah! Where does my free will come in? I can choose for or against God . . . and after that I have had it? I can choose to sit down or stand up, or some other irrelevant things like that? What does it mean to have a free will when things happen to me out of nothing, unexplainable to myself? I must have "faith"? Even if I were to say "yes," I am building on a particle of faith so small it isn't funny.

How would it be if I were to be able to close a door behind me and enter a world of faith? However, where I live there are "legitimate doubts"—"skepticism"—"open-mindedness"—there are anthropological gods, and sublimation—there are self-fulfillment and self-deception . . . there are . . . so many doubts, and so many are so much part of me, always nagging, ridiculing me, defacing me, pulling the rug out from under me. And I am staking everything on a grain of faith?

Maybe my doubts protect me. Maybe my intuition is true: it isn't possible to believe, fully—and live my own life!

And then, if I don't have faith, why should I care! Why don't I just walk out, and leave the matter at that? But that, you see, I can't! There are just too many contradictions for me to deal with. "Duality," it is called? What do I do? Throw out half of myself? Superimpose the two pictures?

Jung, in an article "The Stages of Life," talking about the processes involved in solving problems particular to the stages of life (problem solving seen as steps forward in consciousness), uses the term "a dualistic phase":

> Resorting to psychological terms we would say: the state induced by a problem—the state of being at variance with oneself—arises when, side by side with the series of ego contents, a second series of equal intensity comes into being. This second series, because of its energy value, has a functional significance equal to that of the ego complex; we might call it another, second ego which in a given case can wrest the leadership from the first. This brings about . . . an awareness of one's divided state; it is a dualistic phase (*Modern Man in Search of a Soul*, Harcourt, Brace and World).

Jung is not asking, but I am asking: Who and what is this "Other Energy"?

It is as if all that happened in the past and all that happens in the future is only a slow-motion picture deceiving us into thinking in terms of a stretched-out-existence, whereas our thinking would be closer to reality if our mind were capable of focusing, bringing all that happened and happens, and ever will happen—all eternity . . . into a timeless "Now."

*January 26*　　　Last Sunday two of the kids carried on this exciting conversation about Truth—the truth as we see it subjectively, as opposed to an objective Truth. Does it exist? The older one has "an open mind" and is a self-professed agnostic. His sister suspects the truth as we see it is necessarily subjective.

"What would you do," she challenged her brother, "if one day you knew you had found The Truth?"

"Eat chicken for dinner," he answered, smiling apologetically.

*January 30*　　　I am reading Aschenbrenner's "Conciousness Examen," an exercise "aimed at developing a heart with a discerning vision."

> The examen is not simply a matter of a person's natural power of memory and analysis. . . . It is a matter of Spirit-guided insight into my life and courageously responsive sensitivity to God's call in my heart . . . seeking . . . appreciative insight into the mystery which I am.

> This . . . presumes that we have become sensitive to our interior feelings, moods, and slightest urgings and that we are not frightened by them but have learned to take them very seriously. It is here in the depths of our affectivity, so spontaneous, strong, and shadowy at times, that God moves us and deals with us most intimately. These interior moods, feelings, urges, and movements are the "spirits" that must be sifted out, discerned, so that we can recognize the Lord's call to us at this intimate core of our being.

It is time for me to start "listening."

*January 31*

I am mistaken assuming that this inner "desire" has anything at all to do with spirituality. I am just plain lonesome. To treat the symptoms as if they represented a religious need is deceiving myself. It makes me wary—wary—wary. For sure I am motivated by self-interest. I just want to be happy.

At the same time, there is such a sense of truth about the moments I know better—I cannot afford to throw out the baby with the bathwater. I know there is no other way than His way. But . . . how much of me is interested in that truth?

Is my "discernment" going to be able to reach beyond my sense of loneliness?

I guess there is a way: through the loneliness. All these bits of wisdom! And then what!

*February 3*

The truth is that whenever I do try to pray across this immeasurable distance, the only answer I get back is, "Get on with your work"—"Communicate with people"—"Stick to the human side of the business."

How I hate work (housework)! How utterly useless and senseless it seems to me! How second grade and inferior to "the spiritual life." And how mistaken I seem to be, feeling this way!

*February 8*

"What is keeping me away?" I was thinking this morning in church. Symptomatic of how far out of line I really am is the fact that I have no sense of wrong, no awareness of any concrete guilt. Just a blindfolded rage at being a failure. "Let us remind ourselves of our sins," they say before the Mass. And I am ignorant. I can look back and through myself and be numb—all I see is grey—undefined diffused spiritual illiteracy.

"Thy kingdom come," we pray—and we are expecting this "utopia" to come about sometime here on earth? If not for ourselves, at least for our children's children's . . . children . . . ? What did He say though? "My kingdom is not of this world"—and we are interpreting that to mean that this kingdom is an invisible spiritual sovereignty which exists independent of our material world. . . . I wonder? Maybe this kingdom which is already "in existence" "now," which is "unseen" and "unknown" to us . . . which "conquers death" . . . is in fact the kingdom of life-after-death. Is it? The thought scares me.

> For He must be king until He has put all His enemies under His feet . . . and the last of the enemies to be destroyed is death . . . (1 Cor 15:25–26).

If that doesn't sound as though the only way into His kingdom is through death! Why does this scare me so? Is a guilty conscience tugging at my soul, because I feel myself trying to be clever, giving new meaning to unthought of ideas? I am not really trying to be clever though. This Kingdom has been on my mind. Mostly so because I understand it to be Jesus' Kingdom—and Jesus has so little appeal! Just look at the map of world religions! So how is this Kingdom ever going to come about?

I know I am self-oriented,
so I pray
not to be so.
I know that for all practical purposes
I am not interested in doing His will . . .
and if I look at myself
and see what is wrong,

I think:
"So what!" . . .
and I pray—not to be so!

But what if my prayer gets answered—
then what?
I am getting myself deeply involved on a road of no return.
Once I see—myself
and what I could be,
I will have run out of excuses.

I am scared!


February 21

This is the Kingdom of God:
God's power
in all people
at all times
to negate evil
and turn it into Good.


March 1

"You did not choose me, no, I chose you . . . " (Jn 15:16).
This is the statement I have objected to more than to any
other. I don't like a preferential God, who "chooses." But in
fact that is the truth. It isn't that I can choose for myself a
vantage point from which I can manage a commitment—the
commitment has been made "for" me!

This does-and-does-not take into account the fact that in
the future anything can happen—and this does-and-does-not
take into account all the questions I have for which I have not
found an answer. The commitment has been done for me;

however, it is I who have to give definition and form to it in the realities of my life. . . .

I suppose only God can do something once and for all. Our "once and for all" involves a lifetime of ups and downs. We live in time. Stretched out time.

*March 6*

I don't think I have ever in my life employed my will against my inclinations. If I ever considered sacrifice, it was only as long as I "felt like it." Only now am I beginning to see my will as something which can be turned against me, however reluctantly so and screamingly uncooperative. It is possible for me to intend to do that what every fiber inside me refuses to do . . . and pray . . . how much I pray. . . . If I think how much of me is involved in this colossal effort to deny myself something so ridiculously little . . . how little does that make me! How pathetically little.

I just think of the poor widow in the Bible who offered her two small coins in the temple—and Jesus saw her and praised her, because "she gave from her poverty." God knows I should not be as poor as I am—but I am. . . .

And then there is my son who asks: "How would you like to be completely self-actualized right this moment?"

I tore out the previous page. Thinking to, maybe, share this writing has made me altogether too clever. With an audience reading over my shoulder I am self-conscious—and unless I can regain my integrity and write with the honesty I feel in prayer, these thoughts become a farce.

✳

Yesterday I read. I put in an absolute minimum as far as the family was concerned and read from morning to midnight. It is the usual procedure: I read—fighting off a growing guilt feeling and emerge at the end of the book with a brooding temper—which makes me feel guilty—which makes me decide I am in no position to pray, because I knew all along it was going to end up this way and I didn't do anything to change course—or stop—so if I am cut off it is my own fault and there I am cut off. . . .

I suppose, technically, this is called neurotic behavior— and the guilt is neurotic. Thinking about this now, I realize that my guilt feelings kind of arrive on cue—unrelated to a conscious decision and absolutely unrelated to a sense of sorrow. I'll avoid the behavior, to avoid the hangover of guilt—not because I relate my action to other people or even to myself. My "good" and my "bad" are conditioned—they are a-moral.

I have been praying, "Help me see through the grey— help me see my sins for what they are—and (because I badly need to learn to see that too) help me see the good as clearly good in me." Is this the beginning of a glimmer of light, knowing I have to see beyond my guilt-feelings?

On one hand, I don't think my conscience is so underdeveloped. In many ways I can see clearly. I can see "in theory." I can see when I am faced with "an issue." It is where I act habitually that the red and green lights of my conscience are automated by some conditioned force unrelated to me . . .

and I stop and go without thinking. I feel in many ways I have
hardly grown up!

*March 19*          My morality is completely self-centered.
My criteria are mine.
My norms, standards and principles are self-fabricated.
And my "sins"
are failures in view of my own expectations.

That is why my "guilt" does not lead to sorrow.

And in this context
who is to forgive me?

*March 28*          Is the human condition as it is,
giving us a choice between heaven or hell,
and is Christ showing us the way?
Or would there have been no heaven to begin with
without Him?
In other words:
Is Christ our Guide or our Redeemer?

A sacrilegious question:
Why do we need a Redeemer?

I do not fathom sin!

Maybe I can't "understand" sin because I don't want to accept the fact that I do sin. Even writing this down cringes my insides. All I want to do is run!

The kids once asked me if it was a sin to take drugs. They were dead-serious and I beat around the bush in a magnificent way. While I was talking, I knew I was wrong—but I kept talking . . . and I'll never forget the nonsense I threw up.

Adam and Eve ran away. How can I stand up and say, "Yes, I did!" If, upon accepting the responsibility for my sins, I am not given a sense of sorrow and forgiveness, I will die.

I think, up to now, I have not ever fully accepted responsibility for the wrong committed. So far, I have made every "sin" so complicated, so clouded over with extenuating circumstances, the act so far removed from an only partially conscious decision, somewhere way down the line of a chain reaction of events . . . that the guilt was too diffused to pinpoint. It was practically not there. And I got off beyond the reach of blame.

My God, how am I to stand up—and if I do, please, don't make me stand there like a statue; give me the sense, please, to see my wrong in relation to You—and tell me how to ask for forgiveness.

And I am not talking about being repelled by the "connotation" of sin either—I am talking about what sin constitutes.

I admit I have made the wrong decisions sometimes, but who has a clear picture of all the alternatives all the time?

I have made mistakes—but that is "only human," isn't it?

I have done "wrong"—but wrong is socially and culturally defined, and ambiguous, to say the least.

Sin is something of quite a different order—to accept responsibility for that. . . .

I am numb.

<table>
<tr><td>

*April 18*

</td><td>

Even if I were to leave the past for what it is, assuming that it is of no use to mourn over sins retrospectively—even if I were to consider only the present—and accept responsibility for what I do now—I cannot live my life subject to sin. It is deadening.

However, telling myself that I cannot live that way doesn't make me feel any nearer to the truth. Somehow, accepting the responsibility for sin, regardless of the circumstances, leaves me with a much more authentic sense of reality than admitting that I can't live with them, and that therefore it can't be "all that bad" and that we probably don't commit as many sins as the books like us to believe.

Maybe—in spite of the fact that I accept responsibility,
I don't have to live with sin,
because
Christ has "taken away the sins of the world,"
they say.
How?
"Through His cross"—they say.

It is absolutely beyond me.

</td></tr>
</table>

If I do accept responsibility,
a blanket responsibility covering all and everything,
unthought-out,
unquestioned,
because there is absolutely no other way out,
if I accept responsibility and leave it at that,
without relating my sins—to God,
without, in fact, another care in the world other than admitting
that I can and have committed a wrong which technically—
they say—
"offended" (?) God,
without me understanding that this is so,
without a true sense of sorrow,
then
will that truly be enough
for the time being?

Or am I opting for an emotional catharsis?
Am I expecting my soul to take flight
and find some mystical solution somewhere,
after the responsibility is accepted?

In all honesty
and for the sake of integrity of faith,
can I forget that all this has to make sense to me,
because sin first of all supposes I have some "sense"
and, more important,
that all this:
sin, responsibility, and guilt,
is beside the point
without sorrow.
. . .
And where am I to get sorrow, if I don't understand?

*April 30*        Watching myself solve the ethical and moral questions in my
life is like watching an accomplished lawyer in a court of law.
My judgments follow lines of responsibility—accountability—
liability. . . . I am ignorant of love and unable to authentically
care for the ones concerned in the case.

        We are facing a family "suit."

           The issue: sexual freedom.

           The complication: possible pregnancy.

           The question: to use or not to use contraceptives.

           Relevant data: the parties concerned are under-age.

        And I am solving this whole "problem" by remote
control, long-distance from an inner self which is not involved
in the case. I don't "care" in the true sense of the word.

*May 1*        I am going to have to allow myself to be loved—in order to
learn to love.

*May 2*        "To have a good . . . relationship,
each must strive to be responsive to the other,
not responsible for the other" (Masters and Johnson, *The
Pleasure Bond*).

And I have been raised in terms of responsibility!

*May 4*        I wonder
if the death
of the Son of God
on the cross
would have

redeemed us,

. . .

without the Eucharist?


*May 16*      For me
to ever again
think of sin
without,
first, centering myself in the love of God,
and,
second, acknowledging the redemption,
would make my life so unreal it isn't funny.
Whether or not I "understand" the redemption
is beside the point.
Whether or not I "see" any connection
between Jesus' death and my sins being "taken away"
is irrelevant.
To keep myself at a distance from the person of Christ
because "I don't understand,"
or because I want to ask the questions—"objectively,"
is not only conceited and arrogant,
it is also depriving myself of the only way to know Him,
which is to live with Him.
Let us say that I have asked the questions "in good faith."
This is no longer so.
Given the reality of sin,
there is no way I can function unless I am redeemed.

In sin—we are—dead.
If I have been told a hundred thousand times
that sin means death,
a hundred thousand times I have thought
that this was so metaphorically speaking only!

That isn't so.
It is the hard—cold—truth.
Now, I know that I am not dead.
I am alive.
Very much so.
And if I have been told that this "life" in me
is "the life of Christ,"
I have thought that many times: "Oh, well. . . . "

I want to be aware of being redeemed.
I want to be aware of this life in me.
I don't want to break my head
or my heart
or my soul
over my sins,
because
in a sense
they are irrelevant.
What matters is
how we live with the fact that we are sinful,
how we allow for the life of Christ
exactly there, where we are sinful.
What matters is. . . .
It has all been said
so many times
and in so many ways
before. . . .
If it would be true, for me . . . please. . . .

" . . . through Jesus Christ, Your Son . . . "—we say.
And I always thought this was an "afterthought"!
How am I going to say it enough times,
to make up for all the times
I didn't know what it was all about?
And even saying it now—thinking that I "know,"

I don't know. . . .
I have kept myself at a distance—and here I am
at a distance.
The "Life of Christ" is an unknown entity to me.

I am going to have to reread that Bible again.

If we paid as much attention to Pentecost,
as we do to Christmas
and Easter,
we would be ahead.

I am angry these days
and frustrated,
tense,
off balance. . . .

I have a sense
of being somewhere, and
I don't know where.

I feel
as if I have walked into a room
and the room is empty
although I can feel the presence of
someone who has just left. . . .

I am angry,
but
the things I am angry with
are not the ones I am angry with.

I feel
"about to . . . "
but
"what" escapes me.

This is the point where I easily feel "guilty."
I want to know
the cause of my uneasiness
and I assume
habitually so
that I have done "something wrong."

This is not so—
God knows it is not so—
at least not intentionally so . . . or knowingly so
and I am not about to embark on a psychological dig,
I tell myself!

Of all the reasons I can think of
for being at odds with myself,
none is as authentic as the one that tells me
I am ahead of myself.
I have left half of myself behind.
I have made gigantic steps
and I have left half of myself behind.
If I have learned there is only one way—His way,
I find that in an effort to focus on this truth
I have cultivated in myself a one track mind.
I am becoming intolerant.
If I was blind before
and thought I'd learned to see,
I am still blind.
I have only changed focus.
Not enlarged my vision.

Maybe it is good
summer is coming,
because
more than anything else,
I need time.


*May 29*

Any experience
that is enriching
leaves you
with the capacity
to be
that
much
more
lonely!

I wonder . . . I wonder . . .
As long as I feel as
distant
as I do,
I will never ever experience sin
as a "breakdown" of a relationship.
I am unrelated to begin with!


*June*

I am angry, I have said.
I feel as if in the process of "finding myself"
I am peeling off protective layers.
. . . .
The anger,
the disturbing anger,
I find

is a part of me, I have laid bare.
It isn't a "reaction."
It is me!

I got the car scratched,
just because I wasn't going to be pushed off the road!
It makes me feel an adolescent again
remembering times long ago.

What do they say?
You have to "channel" your instincts?
Humm!!

*June*          Interesting! I am reading De Mello, *A Way to God:*

> Sometimes this exercise (exercises of body
> awareness) will result in an opening up of the
> unconscious and so you may be flooded with strong
> feelings and fantasies connected with repressed
> material, generally feelings and fantasies connected
> with sex and anger. There is really no danger here at
> all, provided you continue with your awareness
> exercises and give no importance or attention to the
> fantasies and feelings.

So it all follows a pattern, does it?

*June 15*      From this morning's sermon:
                "We learn to love through faith and reconciliation."
How? How? How?
. . . .

And suppose I don't have to know how.
Suppose I just need faith
and reconciliation.

I am tired of asking questions.

*June 19*    He calls me friend . . . but in my vocabulary the word "friend"
covers a multitude of sins. In a relationship which becomes too
uncomfortably close it is a convenient word to create a
protective distance . . . and in a relationship which is stand-
offish and formal it is a nice word to create an illusion of
closeness. . . . At best, "friend"-ship is ambiguous, and as they
say in Dutch: "Een goede buur is beter dan een verre vriend"
(A good neighbor is better than a distant friend).

*July 3*    Maybe I have been praying for the wrong thing.
Maybe,
instead of praying to know my sins,
to know sorrow for them,
to . . . ?
My G., what a blank my head is these days.
I feel sick. Not just down, but sick.
Maybe
I ought to pray to know His Peace
when it is right in front of me.
I am sure I am staring right at it
not seeing.
What does de Mello say in his *Way to God?*
"The enjoyment of His peace is an acquired taste."
I suppose peace and love and happiness
I disagree with on principle.

At best I consider them the fringes of reality
not to be taken too serious in the business of daily living.
I have no taste for them.
. . . .

Not that I haven't known peace—or joy.
I have.
But I just wait for it to go away
because I know it will.
It always does.
It never lasts.
It isn't anywhere near as reliable and dependable
as the misery in my life
and I'd rather be realistic.
My G., how I opt for misery!
Choose it,
create it,
see it—all around me, wherever it is
or isn't
or might be!
I've got to shift gears.

I've got to shift gears,
change focus.

Please,
give me the grace,
Your Grace,
to believe in the possibility
. . . .
the real-life-possibility
. . . .
of Your Peace.
A lasting peace?

If my prayer has a question mark,
it isn't that I doubt.
It's just that I don't know,
don't know with my soul-self
anything
about anything
of the good things in life.

I have never asked for them either, have I?

*July 5*

What people "see" isn't determined by what they look at, but by what they look with. When I first met the man who calls me friend, I was attracted because he was "not there"—he, as a person, withdrew from the scene to allow me an unobstructed "encounter with God." (This "encounter," by the way, is a big word for a very tentative searching on my part.) When the kids first met him, their reaction was: "He is a weak man. He hides behind his religion and behind his 'God' and behind his being a priest." Remarkably, we experienced more or less the same thing, but explaining this to ourselves, we interpreted it in different words. Why? Because we looked with different eyes.

*July 8*

If I could keep a wordless diary I would; nothing I write seems to touch spirituality—nothing spiritual (?) in my life survives words.

I wish I could pray on paper. I need much to confirm the prayerful desire (?) in me to become other-directed—not to become aware of "self" (de Mello), but to become aware of the "subtle and profound ways of the Lord deep in our hearts"—to confront myself, yes, but "in Christ, before the Father"—to become "discerning" and "responsive"; all

Aschenbrenner's vocabulary, but more than anything else, it fits me.

It sounds so unworldly and not "with it" to want to do "the will of God"—but that is what I want to do. Why? (Here I am talking to myself again, and "thinking," instead of praying.) I want to do so, because in my prayerful self this is what I need to do. This is what I pray to do. And not really in an emotional dreamy heavenly way—but in my life of every day and in my relationship with those nearest to me. This is why I need the discernment—this is why I need to allow myself the responsiveness. There is no way I can impose upon myself a new way of living—I have to start from the inside out. "Please, be with me."

*July 14*        Participation in the Mass
doesn't even demand
our sacrifice,
only
the "work of human hands."

*July 17*        Remember the islands
and the unbelievably beautiful aquarium fishes in the Gulf,
and my observation to a family friend,
"Why are they so beautiful if we can't even see them?"
"For themselves," he said.

I think I have been taught
that the earth was created "for us"—
for us to enjoy
for us to use
for us to own?

God created the earth—and everything on it
and Adam "named" all the animals.

The story of creation tells much about God's power
and might
and care
and much about man's "dominion,"
but never, ever, in all my life have I been told
that the birds
and the bees
and the trees
have a "life" of their own,
a value in themselves.

We talk about "conservation," yes,
because if we don't, we won't "have" it anymore—later.
We talk about "reverence for life"—yes—human life!
But considering the values of life-on-earth
the scales tip in favor of man,
so much so
and so routinely so
and so "justifiably" so
that we forget and take the universe for granted.

*July 20*
Went to the local church today with one of the kids and it happened to be the feast day of the Holy Redeemer. The church is a Redemptorist church. The theme of the sermon: Christ the Redeemer. Faith.

The more that goes on in my soul, the more I feel handicapped by a language that doesn't convey my inner life. I just want to remember that it is His feast today. I much would want to lead His life. I am not even asking myself if I believe or not!

28

*July 24*      Our pretty daughter is "searching," hunting around the city
             for "the light," and came home with another book. The
             subject: meditation, mind development, "awareness."

> Mind cultivation is suitable to every one without
> exception. Be always aware and mindful and follow
> by practicing the simple instructions given here and
> see by experiencing the changes that come about;
> even your best friends will notice.

What is the difference between this "awareness" and the
awareness De Mello speaks about? If this book can "straighten
out" people, what is it that I am doing? Maybe that is the
wrong question again. Maybe the object of religion isn't "to
straighten out" people? I am still looking in the wrong
direction. How many times does it come to me in my prayer
that the only thing I have to do on this earth is bring honor
and glory and praise to God . . . not by being perfect, but by
being exactly what I am—now.

*July 31*      If I were a millionaire, I'd shop in the Far East.
             The silk prints are exquisite,
             the pottery I fell in love with years ago,
             and the jewelry. . . .

             But picking the stuff up—and out of the Orient—
             bringing it home,
             is like collecting wildflowers
             and putting them in a vase
             on the kitchen table.

This "good life" is catching up with me. I sit down at table and overeat. This bothers me for several reasons. I don't feel good, physically. It doesn't do my figure any good, and I am walking around with a nagging guilt feeling, nurtured by injured pride, because I just cannot "take it or leave it." I am just about at the mercy of something as lowly and unspiritual as food. Somewhere, in the depth of my soul, I also know that I am walking a tightrope and that this indulgence is asking for "real trouble."

The problem is that I feel quite alone in my half-hearted campaign to "be good"—as if the issue were not whether or not I indulge myself, but, rather, what do I do with myself and my guilt feelings after I indulge. It is as if God is trying to help me make the best of a set-up which is in fact unhealthy. But, I am learning something. Not being able to do what I'd like to do, like being in control of my appetites, is frustrating, to say the least. Accepting myself where I find myself right now, and doing so graciously, is difficult. Not walking out on myself and on my prayer is something I can do only with the grace of God.

I don't know where in the prism of my soul "spiritual well-being" diffracts into a sensation of being on-top-of-the-world, but it does.

If, at the end of a forty day fast, the devil were to tempt me to "tell this stone to turn into a loaf" (Lk 4:1–13), I might not be interested. If he were to offer me the world in return for worshiping him, I don't really think I would fall for that. I am not interested in owning the world, and the idea of worshiping anyone but God seems a ridiculous suggestion. If, however, he were to insinuate that as "a son of God" I might throw myself off this pinnacle because it is written that His angels would protect me, that would be a temptation for me! I can fall for that.

As a child I never understood this temptation. What would be so wrong if the Son of God were to prove He is the Son of God? Intellectually I still don't understand. With my soul's eye, however, I can see myself on the pinnacle and I can see that this particular temptation would throw me very much off balance. I could even jump. But He didn't!

If the word pride comes to mind, it comes from education rather than inspiration. However, in the delicate sensitivity of my soul, I feel as grateful as if I were handed a new life and much conscious of the grace of God that has enabled me to see myself with this tendency. Nor does my soul question the deep spiritual wrong of such a "jump."

*August 18*    I cannot get away from the fact that I have lots of illusions about myself, about other people around me and about relationships—and the word pride looms at the edge of my conscience. Thank the Lord for being gentle with me, for not accusing me or even forcing me to take a stand. Much more gentle than I am with myself is this inner confidence, turning me away from my own reflective, analytical, self-indulging mind, urging me to love and to rely on Him.

*August 28*    Home again—after six weeks of travel and sending off two kids. Sometimes I wonder. . . .

East is East and West is West and never the twain shall meet?

Sometimes I wonder if the mentality of the East doesn't suit me better. I feel as if life in this aggressive, competitive, self-assertive West brings out the worst in me. If only the cultured gentleness of the East didn't smooth over so much hidden cruelty and materialism. If I could choose the best of two worlds I would wish for what I, as a Western world woman, would understand integrity to be—softened and made truly honorable by Eastern gentleness and respect.

*August 29*

And then there is our democratic dream of "equality" and equal "rights"—"rights" that in our society have come to mean "the right" to as big a car and as big a house and as long a vacation. In a country with socialized medicine, standard education, and equal rights proclaimed from the rooftops, privileges don't exist.

I think of the East which bows to a class system, which is burdened by its poor, where servants work and pay obeisance to their masters, where there is a constant need to be aware of one's position in relation to others—and then, when I think of this great amorphous Western society where all are "equal," I wonder.

I wonder about Hong Kong airport and Tokyo airport and Fiumicino airport and the airport of Seattle. You would never know where you had landed unless they told you so. There is a TV in every airport, with the same music. There are the same high-rises and the same unconcern among city people. Whatever made the East think they had anything to gain from Western ways? Why is it that in our moments of truth, when we see most clearly the righteousness of an idea—in this case: equality—why, at that very moment and in the same breath, do we corrupt it?

Yes, we have equal rights, but once this is said and done, I feel I have lost footing with the very principle I proclaim. I feel as if, more essential than our claim to fill a need, is our need. I feel as if, were we to follow this drive toward "equal rights," we would find ourselves midstream, leading into no-man's land. I almost feel as if this luring, shining symbol of Equality is the most subtle temptation in our lives, and a most insidious way of making us believe something which is not.

*August 31*  Just guess what the liturgy of this morning's Sunday Mass was about? About pride and humility. The first Sunday back home I have to hit it just right! Pride—the capital sin—the origin behind a multitude of other sins—and he named them all . . . and humility—really "nothing more than the truth about oneself" . . .

*September 1*  Just read one of those Reader's Digest stories where someone performs a brain operation, for the first time in his life, getting the medical instructions over the phone. I would not have operated. I would have let the boy die.

How much of our humility depends on our self-confidence? What comes first, really . . . the humility or the self-confidence?

*September 2*  Lack of self-confidence
is only a perverted upside-down sense of pride.
It starts with the same premise:
"I" as the center of my universe
and it regards everything and everyone as a threat
to that status.

It is what I call the "unwritten-pages" in my life that have been truly significant. It is what I don't write about that has made the difference: an awkward, hesitant sense of consciousness which operates at a level beyond words; "decisions" and "clarifications" at an inner level so unnatural to me that they scared me. And I do mean "scared me"— scared me to a point of physical fear; scared me enough to make me wonder whether this "other mind" of mine wasn't operating on the verges of a psychological idiosyncrasy; scared me enough to confirm my suspicion that I would be better off without these "experiences."

Not so. I am better off with them. The more I actually allow myself to be directed at this level and the more this consciousness becomes part of my normal life, the less I have to "put up" with it.

Now, more than ever, I would like this writing to be prayerful. It is a confession I cannot formally make right now, but I need very much to declare myself.

I have always thought I led a decent Christian life. My "sins" were more like "slips of the tongue" and could mostly be "explained" in terms of tiredness, misunderstanding or as the natural result of our imperfect human condition. My attitude, if the unavoidable had to happen, was, "So what?" An apology was, according to my inner "integrity," usually out of order. At the very best I could offer an excuse.

If, recently, I "accepted" the sins of my life, I accepted them as unavoidable. I so much as said, "Yes, I did make a slip of the tongue," rather than saying, "Well, considering appearances I must have made a slip of the tongue." If I had an inkling of the disintegrating effect of sin, it was only from the point of view that I, having my salvation in mind, could not afford that kind of disintegration—and so, obviously, I needed a figure such as Christ. It was a calculated need, deprived of any sorrow. What mattered to me was that I needed to "save my soul."

Confront Jesus on the cross—and give my sins to Him? "Outrageous," I thought. "First of all, how do I know if I believe in Him. Second . . . ?" I knew there was another reason, but I didn't know what it was. Some inner good sense told me it was essential to clear up this situation, only to find myself incapable . . .

Here I have become reflective . . . and far from prayerful . . . Please . . . I need this confession, to be made in your presence . . . I have found my "second reason" . . . You have pointed it out to me.

My "sins" are no incidents, or an occasional malfunctioning of an otherwise well-balanced, religiously oriented personality. My sin is as deeply ingrained and as totally part of me as the salt is in my body. There is nothing I say, and nothing I do, that is not contaminated and distorted by the same pride that left me standing there "in front of the cross," indignant at the outrageousness of a surrender . . .

*September 4*

No matter how truly good it is to be fully human—and only human—I feel most real and most at peace with myself there where I have been so reluctant to go . . . and aware of the fact that everything I am and everything I have has been given me with God's favor and God's love.

If this need to be "restored" is truly inspired by God, don't let me ever lose it. But don't let me ever delude myself into thinking that needing to be in His presence could camouflage an escape.

How often do I pray, "I detest all my sins because of Thy just punishments"—and how often have I thought, how is God tabulating our "punishments"? How are we in the hereafter, or anywhere, going to get through our just quantum of "punishment"?

Now I rather think that the punishment of our sins is instantaneous. They are so much part-and-parcel of the sin—and of our life—that we consider it "normal" to be blind, to be locked up in ourselves, to be at war with the world around us, to go to pieces, to drag ourselves along through the slums of our existence. Instead, we are meant to see; and we are living more in accordance with our true nature if we do "see."

And if I find within myself all the discordant colorings of what we consider the inescapable woes of human life, I have deserved them.

I have never understood how Peter,
having been warned,
could go out and deny the Lord three times.
It is because we don't relate our actions to anything beyond us.

And maybe it wasn't an unkindness on the part of Jesus
to ask Peter, three times over:

"Peter, do you love me?"

Jesus must have known the sorrow in Peter's heart
and the terrible need he felt to confirm his love,
yes,
three times over,
in acknowledgement of his guilt.

*September 7*    I don't have to do anything other than the ordinary
without ever forgetting
that all in the same breath
I can set out
on the road
and be saved,
like Lot's wife (Gen 19:2–6)
and turn into a pillar of salt . . .
because I just cannot resist looking back
and follow my interests
rather than His.

*September 8*    Thus are the moments of truth of four o'clock in the morning.
Now, with all this said and done, I realize that in spite of the
beauty and relevance of the experiences of the past few weeks,
I am not one inch ahead of the man who loves his wife and
works in the rice paddies. To see and feel and know as I have
been able to has been a gift of God—and, like all His gifts, it
has been good. However, this new "faculty," if I could call it
that, is not a sign of holiness. Nor is it, by itself, going to make
me holy. It is frightening to realize that all goodness can
become corrupted, just as love can become possessive—not
only so in theory, but in my own life. I realize with fear and
trepidation that I am inclined to carry my self-indulgence into
every sphere of my life, and corrupt the very best things that
ever happen to me.

Please keep my head together, and my soul truly in Your
peace.

And so, here I am, back full circle—what to do with myself after I fail? Already the terminology gives me away: "I fail!" For the moment all the levers of my soul are on "Hold." Any more current and I'll capsize.

I have these days not been able to allow myself the closeness in prayer that I normally try to look for. Usually I don't pray into space. I hope to pray in some intimacy or with some sense of "contact." These days, praying, I "keep a distance." In fact, even though I am occupying myself with prayer, I keep my eyes wide open, aware of the ordinary living things around me. If I don't, I feel I am in danger of losing myself. If I don't, I feel I could slide into a state of mind which accelerates into an awareness which scares me. There is no real peace of mind there, only turmoil. And if an "awareness" of God, in prayer, is to lead to peace, then I question this tumultuous association with prayer.

I am asking myself: Have I been indulging in seeking the effects of a real closeness, which was there, and is the indulgence now breaking up on me? Is it maybe natural or to be expected that a normal human being somehow goes off-balance for a while in the after-effects of a "real experience"? Am I just struggling with the moods of the calendar or a depression related to my age or heaven knows what? Still believing in some "reality" of my "discernment"—originally— somewhere (and I think I know exactly where), where did this reality leave off and the repercussions begin? Am I right in avoiding the turmoil? Or should I face the storm because obviously there are so many things in me absolutely and totally in contradiction with a "presence of God" that there cannot be anything but turmoil when I try to meet Him in prayer? And back again, full circle, am I trying to meet Him or do I only like to look at myself? Why should I try to "discern" His will . . . His presence . . . His . . . whatever, if in fact it makes no difference at all? It would be better if I swept the floor and left these matters at rest. What motivates me anyway to wear myself out as I am doing?

I know one thing though. If anyone were to tell me to stop trying, I could not. And more important, I would not! I am . . . stuck, I guess. I much regret the illusions, the allusions, the pretensions, all the unrealness, which is my contribution to this "dialogue," which is beyond me; I can cry my heart out for every aspect and every coloring which reflect my sin, but . . .

*Set me like a seal on your heart,*
*like a seal on your arm.*
*Song of Songs 8:5*

*September 10, 1980*   I don't understand myself. It isn't that I am insensitive. I am not. The difficulty lies with the emotions involved in relationships. I don't experience myself as "caring" for other people. The only possible way for me to care would be in response to someone who truly cares for me . . . or to somehow "borrow" from God's love for people, which makes me feel quite cheap. I ought to love people for themselves— not because in a roundabout way I can try to move into the stream of God's love and then employ His love "second-hand." Genuine love escapes me. Sin and sorrow have magnitude only at the times that I am faintly or fervently aware of a relationship. How I envy people who are genuinely moved by or to others, those who seem to be naturally loving.

Short of attempting some homespun self-analysis, I wonder if this could be because I don't actually "believe" in tenderness or affection—I am skeptical. The biggest cancer in my soul that I am aware of is a defensive, self-protective, unrelating resistance I feel. I use the word cancer, not sin. It is a sickness. I have often, half-sarcastic, half-hurt, told myself that even in heaven, I would turn around and walk out . . . if anyone were to try to "approach" me. Think about what that means! Maybe, maybe, I could, somehow, readjust my feelings. As it is, they are there.

I wonder if a distortion of such a primary need, the need for a relationship, can hamper one's spiritual development and one's understanding of sin and sorrow?


*September 15*   If I cannot stand to look at myself and see all the many times I "fail," surely it cannot be a solution to close my eyes! If I could only learn to be as gentle with myself as He has been with me!

*September 20*   Read an article in the Gazette yesterday night dealing with depression. It makes me realize how much of my "renewal" this past year has had psychological, therapeutic reasons. "So I have made it," I told myself. I even told myself that now that I have "made it," psychologically speaking, now is the time for me to decide whether or not I want to go on and involve myself in spiritual matters. My God, the arrogance of arrogance! The unbelievable blasphemous pride. As-if-I-could-"decide"! How can I be so obstinately, incredibly, spiritually, ignorant. Maybe if I were empty handed and blind . . . but even that would be too much on which to base my claim . . .

I've got to walk
and keep walking,
and never look back,
and go
one step at the time,
and pray
and pray
and pray . . .

*September 29*   I asked You, "Would You give me the grace to Love?" . . . and You answered, "Are you willing to accept this, what you call 'second-hand' love?" . . . and I resent going elsewhere (in my prayer to God) for something I would prefer to be authentically mine. I resent having to "borrow." I resent the position of dependency. I would like to see myself capable of love all on my own strength!

*October 2*

I am fighting paradoxes, and it isn't until I drop dead in the middle that the two propositions shift into a new perspective, and both become true.

Too bad I can't seem to get at that new perspective without reaching the end of my rope . . . and going blind . . . first.

*October 6*

Read C. S. Lewis', *The Weight of Glory and Other Addresses.* In "Membership" he says, we are "getting the whole picture upside down," starting with the doctrine that every individuality is of infinite value. The value of the individual does not lie within him—he is capable of receiving value. Lewis then talks about "the pestilent notion that each of us starts with a treasure called personality locked up inside him, and that . . . to express this is the main end of life." Contrary to this, Lewis believes that trying to do "any bit of work as well as it can be done for the work's sake" and "the submission of the individual to the function" will bring about the personality. And here I am with my fanatic and treasured faith in the inherent value of the individual!

Maybe it is excusable that I am a child of my time. That I do believe that we attain our development starting "from the inside out." "No," says Lewis, "it will come to us when . . . we have suffered ourselves to be fitted into our places." I do believe life is a question of finding for the individual "a place in the living temple which will do justice to his inherent value and give scope to his natural idiosyncrasy." "No," says Lewis, "there is no such question." The place is there. The man won't be a man until he "fits in." And as for Lewis' suggestion to do "any bit of work for the work's sake," no, I resent that! If I cannot possibly avoid work, I will work for my own beatification! Or, if I am in the mood, for the glory and honor of God.

Thinking about work, and its function, and about having to "fit in," I asked the maid from now on to come only once a week instead of twice, to help me with the little extras. "The work" I will do myself. I told her this is "for financial reasons," which is true also. As for myself . . . in my most obstinate moods, I hate housework with a zealous and holy indignation! Sticking with it will "kill me."

*October 7*

What do I pray for?
I pray for You to help me see my sins—
and I can't stand to see them.
I pray for You to give me the grace of sorrow—
and the sorrow breaks my heart.
I pray to see Your Goodness around me—
and it awakens in me a terrible longing.
What else do I pray for?
I pray for Your Will to be done
and all of my inner self is obscure and incomprehensible.
And if I pray for Your Peace . . . ?
The "further along" I get,
the further I find myself heading the wrong way.
Am I . . . ?
Is it possible for me to "pray" on paper?
Why do I write anyway?
Who or what is benefiting by my writing?
Does the writing prove to myself that I exist?
Think?
Try?
The more I write, the more I am out of touch.
Somebody ought to throw all my pens away.
. . .
I think the one devil that has been cast out
has come back with seven others.

*October 9*        There is the contradiction: the assumption that I am by nature incapable of any sentiment remotely related to love, versus the supposition that I "have to" love—and express love—at a personal level. I am acknowledging in myself two contrary illusions, making allowances for both of them, cutting myself in two . . . and ignoring the fact that I need to love and be loved.

The truth is that I have forgotten my natural talents. Instead I am catering to my hang-ups. I am fighting a self which has come to exist, but which is not me. Me is a person with an inborn sense of beauty—and a fragile need to touch—and an eye for the intangible—and, yes, a talent for the personal.


*October 21*       In love
we are either
"playing with fire"
or
"walking on water" . . .
depending on our point of view.


*October 23*       "I call you friends,
because I have made known to you
everything I have learned from my Father" (Jn 15:15).

Note that He does not say:
"I have told you
everything
because you are my friends."
No,
it is the other way around.
Friendship is not the condition!

*October 24*     Why do I need so much to enter into a personal relationship?
Because there is nothing I can do with all my discoveries
unless I somehow can change. There is no way I can "fight"
my isolation, no way I can avoid sin by concentrating on a
negative not-doing-wrong. I have to do-right, and somehow
my "right," my being truthful about myself, leads me to the
need for a relationship where my real self is involved. But for
that I need someone else!

No reason why this someone else has to be my equal
though! I am beginning to see the fight, the resentment, the
anger, the effort at trying to equalize things, the supposed
need to bring the other down to my level . . . If I am right that
I have to readjust things in my upside down and
"independent" soul, I am going one step too far assuming that
this has to be through a relationship I "can manage." Heaven
knows—and I know—I have to get away from myself.


*October 27*     From a day of recollection, sometime before Easter:

> God doesn't want results.
> He wants your heart.


. . .

My heart is with the results!


*October 28*     This is what happened: I put the soup on the gas, full force,
went upstairs and got involved in reading these notes. All of
them. Then I went downstairs and found the kitchen full of
smoke and the meat burning in the pan. "Well, Tony, this is
great," I heard myself say. "Look at the stupidity of this." I
opened the window, poured water in the pan, and tried to deal

with the situation. While I am writing this, the whole house is hazy, full of watery smoke, and I am clinically interested in my own reactions.

For one thing, I don't think I am going to hell for this. I am not going to pieces. I am not guilt-ridden, denouncing myself for a morbid self-interest, or utter disregard of my duties, unworthy of heaven-knows-what . . . I just burned the meat. Much more than guilty, I feel grateful at the sense of balance and justice I must have found somewhere or other, sometime this past year.

A couple of hours later: Something was wrong though, wasn't there? I knew, when I picked up the books: "No, wait, there is a better time for this," but I put the thought away and started reading. I consciously over-rode the better impulse and did what I wanted, got involved in myself rather than in my work. Without going into a mortifying analysis: I was wrong. Seeing clearly like this, without any thundering clouds of guilt obscuring my vision, I am truly sorry. Not so much for burning the meat. Not even so much for the self-indulgence. I am sorry for not "listening."

*October 30*       If at any time, with the house still full of smoke, anyone of my beloved family had walked in and had started criticizing me, things would have been different. I never would have found my way, past all my defenses, back to the point of being sorry. There is quite a difference between me dealing with myself, and someone else dealing with me. I suppose the question is whether they are in a position to do so?

*November 1*      I don't, like C. S. Lewis, put my faith all on the side of reason, and "opposed in battle" to emotion and imagination. I suppose it is a woman's privilege to enjoy the benefits of a functional emotional life. It is my reason that questions, yes, but hardly ever does it supply me with the answers; they come out of nowhere—carried on a silver platter of imagination—and it is my feeling that tells me the platter is for me.

*November 3*      He calls me friend . . . and he says,
"All love comes from God,
whether we are aware of this or not."

*November 4*      I am reading *Theology and Spirituality* by John Dalrymple:

> The root of all sin is that fear in us of being committed, the innate desire to remain shut within ourselves, the refusal to take root in the not-I. . . . We grow in our humanity if we adopt an open attitude toward other people, ready to take the risk of going out to them, to be decentralized, love them. . . .
>
> Self-denial is . . . the built-in safeguard and condition of that love. Without it, love does not dwell in a man, but only possessiveness, and all he does, even his religious acts, will turn to self-advancement.

And I have been haggling with myself about the difference between "self-denial" and "dieting," and I have talked myself out of the denial for fear I would be merely dieting. Well, so much for that.

*November 6*    I am afraid of a relationship, mostly because I don't trust
myself being capable of the necessary detachment. I have a
system of brakes and emergency brakes working that
practically immobilizes me.

To be sure, the relationships I am used to don't give me
much experience. My friendships are basically non-involved—
and if I ever do stick out my neck for someone, it is because I
want to. Maybe the nearest I get to non-possessive love is with
the kids. However, much of these relationships works itself out
on the natural level. It is natural for a mother to love—and it is
just as natural for children to "detach" themselves.

But, to "take pleasure in loving other people," to
"exercise our desires for union with other men and women" (I
am still reading Dalrymple), to enjoy a "sincere and warm
attachment," and yet remain "detached," is about as
paradoxical as one can get, and as unnatural to us as walking
on water.


*November 6*    Finished John Dalrymple. I want to "go home." Back to the
womb, I mean. All the way back where I came from. Listen to
this:

> Fulfillment of the life of grace, however, is not
> achieved without a further crisis which centers this
> time around the mind or will, or deepest self, in man.

> It is a purification of loving. . . . after all our motives
> go dead.

> It is a purification of hoping . . . after we undergo
> "death of self-confidence."

> It is a purification of believing . . . after our faith has
> disappeared into thin air.

My goodness . . . It is a good thing we don't have to live our whole life in the time span of one split second. Thank God for time! And thank God for the fact that for all the time in the world we have, the only moment we have to deal with is right now. A now which has its blessed limitations!

And while I am at it, thank God for the people in this world who write books!

*November 10*    Sometimes I think
God doesn't want our heart as much as He wants our will.
For who can actually rule his heart?
If my heart flutters like Elizabeth's unborn child (Lk 1:41),
or if it drops dead to the bottom of my soul,
what am I to do, other than let it be?

*November 10*    It is much more difficult to take it or leave it than it is to simply abstain; and it is much easier not to love than it is to love without possessiveness. I just wonder what it would have been like to be one of His friends?

Maybe friendship is a male enterprise. Women engage in lots of acquaintances, but by the time a personal relationship becomes meaningful, they operate on a one-to-one basis. They are either all in, or all out. And I am not talking about the exclusiveness of a sexual relationship. I am talking about being claimed by and making claims on another person. I am talking in terms of being meaningful in the life of another—with always the tendency to be "the one." I am not so sure a man tends to make that same claim, but we do, and in a sense we do so rightly.

*November 11*     I won't let any feminist read the previous note!

I am raging a battle on too many fronts:
I am trying to clarify the implications
of this "detached attachment."
I am over my head into the deep water of this course,
"God in Contemporary Writing."
I am doing my work?
Have plenty of time for my family?
Not really spreading my prayer too thin?
But I am not "listening."

It is one thing to write,
and then decide to have someone read what you have written.
It is quite another thing
to write
and have someone read over your shoulder.

*November 17*     About this rediscovery of my natural talents a couple of weeks
ago: that door has been closed so authoritatively and so
definitely, I wonder why it was ever opened. The Lord isn't
interested in what presumably comes to me naturally. He
wants exactly that which I consider impossible—and it seems
that these days more or less everything I touch comes under
that heading.

    Yesterday I knew quite clearly that things are crumbling
under my feet, because He wants it that way. He is—as they
say—a jealous God. And with the outrageousness of a jealous
person, He wants to have it His way, both ways. It isn't

enough that I renounce "the competition," no—I have to walk on the thin ice of His pleasure and let Him deal with it. It isn't enough that I walk out on whatever seems to irk His displeasure, no—I have to keep walking—all the while being vulnerable, all the while exposing myself—and let Him pry me loose of my "attachments" in His own good time.

*November 19*

If I stick with praying the rosary, it is because Mary carried with her a faith in Christ before His teaching was understood . . . before his resurrection . . . before the reassurance of other people who believed what she did. Things must have seemed incongruous to her sometimes!

How I am going to carry with me a belief in holiness in view of the evidence in my life is beyond me too.

*November 21*

I'll have to think, while writing and I have only fifteen minutes to do that in, but let's see.

I am reading Merton's *No Man Is an Island.*

> The man who is selfish, narrow, who loves little and fears much that he will not be loved, can never be deeply sincere. . . . He will deceive himself in his best and most serious intentions. Nothing he says or feels about love, whether human or divine, can safely be believed, until his love be purged at least of its basest and most unreasonable fears. . . .

And I thought that, granted I feel quite incapable of love, at least I was capable of sincerity! I thought that, if all else failed, at least I would have my "inborn" (?) sense of integrity—an integrity which is no effort to me, but rather a need so deeply ingrained I cannot function without it—I thought. Instead, I am deceiving myself? Nothing I have been saying about love—and nothing I feel about love—can even be believed? My battle with love, my skepticism, lack of faith, standoffishness, reluctance—all this and more are evidence of a basic fear that I-will-not-be-loved?

Do I believe God loves me? Yes, I do. To say that He cannot do otherwise seems to put some form of limitation on Him, but I understand that it is in God's nature to love me—no matter what. It is the "no-matter-what" that, somewhere in the corners of my mind, makes His love for me personally insignificant! If He loves me upside down, inside out, black or white . . . what does His love have to do with me? It seems that I don't matter in God's love! I suppose this is one of those statements that would be blasphemous, if I knew what I was talking about. The fact is, I don't. There is a kink in my brain, a missing link in my chain of thought.

Am I to "purge" myself of my "fears"? How? Merton says: "We must strip ourselves of our greatest illusions. . . ." Well—time's up!

✳

I am in deep water and I am going about it the wrong way. For one thing, I am not writing a thesis. I don't have to make sense to anyone other than to myself, and then only after all these disconnected thoughts are brought into focus by some inner experience that changes my way of looking at them.

I know God loves me—personally. To say otherwise would be untrue, unjust and unreal. I also know He loves me "no matter what." . . . The trouble is that somewhere I have it in my little head that love moves between two poles. It doesn't only "move forth," it is also "attracted." Without this "attraction" love in a sense "evaporates." If I follow that line of thought, knowing I am in no way attractive to God—who is sufficient to Himself—then His love for me "evaporates." But, as I said, I know this is not true. I know, by experience, that God's love not only reaches me, but brings me to life.

Why am I breaking my head over this? Because I am still trying to understand non-possessive detached human love, which comes to me "from God," but in the form of "friendship." Maybe, if I were patient, I would do what Merton says:

> Receive this [God's] love in all simplicity [and] the sincerity of [my] love for others will more or less take care of itself.

Maybe I should do just that—and pray. But You have given us a mind to learn to know ourselves. This must be a talent we are to use?

What do I have to understand? Love, which comes to me "from God"—or do I have to understand why it should bother me so much to be at the receiving end of that kind of love? And yes—it does bother me. I cannot do otherwise than accept the fact that God loves me and—once inspired by that love—I not only accept it, I am so deeply and truly grateful for it, that—were it not for my uninspired second thoughts—I would give my life for that Love. However, on the human level it is quite a different matter. Why? Because I am talking about human love which is detached—which does not "need" my response. Where does such a love leave me? In my very best moments, it leaves me with religious resignation. In my worst, it leaves me sterile, debilitated—and in a sense non-existent.

✳

I have torn out two pages because I am not exactly sure I like the implications of my argument. All I know and all I feel is that in a human relationship based on this Godly love,

Charitas, I, at the receiving end, am nowhere! Human love, which doesn't relate to me—for my sake—is somehow objectionable to me.

Now, where did I get lost in this discussion with myself? I say I believe that all love and holiness comes from God and that we are incapable of any love relationship unless we move into the force of God's love. I not only believe that, but I gladly, gladly accept that. How do I reconcile the duplicity: the duplicity of accepting that all love comes from God—and rejecting this love in practice? And just to give myself the benefit of the doubt, just in case the anger of finding myself at the receiving end of such a "Godly affair" has a basis other than hurt pride, let me reformulate the question. Can we truly reconcile these two antagonists: a meaningful human relationship and love which aspires to be detached?

It seems I have moved from an effort of understanding myself to a stance where I am somehow justifiably angry at being hurt. Well, maybe that is the first step: acknowledge the hurt.

I tell myself to use my head and think things out—and when I do, I feel off the track . . . a long way from discernment and prayer . . . and out of touch. I am going to cook the dinner.

*November 22*    It is the lukewarm,
the mediocre,
that moves us into no man's land.

*November 23*     I am beginning to think that the only way to be truly caring
and personal in our relationships is through involving
ourselves in this "objectionable" "borrowed love" I have been
talking about. If all human love thrives on attraction of one
kind or another, much of what is attractive to us is irrelevant!

*November 25*     We are going through the pains of a "terremoto" (earthquake).
So far over three thousand people dead. Why is it that when
people have lost all their possessions, they are somehow
considered less than human?

*November 26*     To be present to God . . .
what does it mean
other than
to be present to our state of life,
to be present to ourselves
and to those around us?
But
doing everything my life requires of me,
making every attempt at being "aware,"
that
in itself
doesn't make me present to God, does it?
. . .
"Look at me," I pray—
as if His mere looking would make me be.

*November 27*     Maybe I am staring myself blind at the fact that our human
affairs never are what they could be. (I am still thinking about
this love-no-matter-what.)

*December 2*

I am at the end of the runway.
I have to either take off—or crash.
The trouble is that all I have is a bit of momentum.
I don't even have my engine into gear!

*December 3*

The Gospel this morning
was about the king arranging this banquet
and no one was interested!
True.
How much I realize I have no taste for His wine.

*December 4*

Maybe the future will tell where I am right now—but I, right
now, don't know. I can hardly believe this venture is dying out
with a sizzle. It isn't fair to judge myself as cold or
disinterested. These are the wrong words. Besides, too much
of what has happened has become authentically mine—I
think? The closest I can get to describing the state of affairs of
my soul is that I am "suspended." I don't know whether the
next move will be up or down—and it doesn't seem relevant,
or interesting to know . . . or important. I feel as if whatever I
expect won't be what I expect—and I feel it is presumptuous
and against the rules of the game to expect anything at all. Any
articulated expectation will only prolong this . . . (?) . . . and
here I go again . . . down, with a sense of "cheating" . . .

Is it so bad to look at myself and see what is going on?
How often have I thought these days that I shouldn't write . . .
Write?
Or write what I am writing?
What is wrong with what I am writing?
Why do I feel dishonest?
. . . .

The truth is that I love You. Anything I say about myself, anything other than that, is escaping or camouflaging the main tendency of my soul. It is the Truth, regardless of the fact that very little in my life speaks of that Truth. It also isn't even remotely sentimental.

If I have basked myself in prayer, sunned myself in what I felt to be God's love, absorbed every ounce of goodness I hoped to come my way, something inside me is now reversing—something inside me is moving out. Maybe the sense of "suspension" is just that: the changing gears. I wonder.

*December 5*

It is as if things are meant to go wrong, as if it were more important to be a fool than to succeed.

What I would like to do is spare myself the day to day decisions, make up my mind once and for all and just-do-it, but . . . when the just-do-it comes around, I decide I have not actually decided yet. Except for the occasional and rare moment my mind never reaches . . . and I act like a fool . . . and then the real thing starts: the issue that seems to matter. Then what?

Is it actually more beneficial for me "to be a fool"? In fact I don't mind, if that is the way it is to be.

*December 8*

The tides of my life,
when all the water
flows
right back where it came from
and my beach is empty,
littered with junk.
And if my soul were to rise again?

Did you ever see the Dutch beaches?
Not like the Mediterranean.
The coast line is so shallow
that when the sea retreats, it goes out for kilometers.
Come to think of it
not all that much washes ashore either.
Not like on the coast of the Pacific Ocean
where my friend collects driftwood,
or like the beach of Chesapeake Bay
where you can find fossils and Indian arrowheads.

I am afraid though
that my personal private beach is littered
and filled with debris.


*December 11*    Today, on the way into town, we passed a "pregnant truck."
In case you don't know what a pregnant truck is, it is the kids'
version of one of those long trailers coming from the Fiat
factory, carrying all colors of little Fiats in its belly.


*December 14*    The trouble is that I steel myself against anticipated criticism—
and then I am stuck with the harness. I am perpetually dealing
across a defensive distance. I wonder. I might be a lot closer to
the truth if I were to stick out my neck and just be vulnerable.
I don't know why our dear Lord is so anxious to have us
"stick out our neck"?


*December 15*    What am I thinking of? Premonitions? I don't know. My
expectations are wordless—but they are expectations!

However, the Lord of my heart seems to be absolutely and totally unconcerned—as if He is waiting for me to unwind so that He can get down to the business of His reality, which not only escapes me but is absolutely beyond me. I always think I do—but I never really do know what He is talking about. And right now I am afraid to pray—to know. Whatever—it doesn't matter. But I pray God that He knows I mean it when I say I am committed—wherever that leads me.

*December 18*

If You are ever thinking of handing me a gift—a real honest-to-goodness-present—how glorious it would be to be able to "externalize" once in a while, just to "come out in the open." It is to my closest friends, in matters that touch me most deeply, that I feel myself in utter contradiction.

What, for heaven's sake, is so disastrous about being affectionate, trustful and "transparent"? I don't care what anyone thinks of me—I say—and I am not half as anxious to hide the malice of my heart . . . but why—why—why—do I violate myself hiding the Good?

*December 20*

If I could be convinced that I am "trying" for ulterior motives, I would drop out of the whole enterprise. The trouble is that in the obscure corners of my brain something is trying to sidetrack me and I might as well consider all those attempts temptations. I know that at the most sincere point in my prayer my intentions are straight. If somewhere on the unconscious level I am deceiving myself, there is nothing I can do about it. You have to do it, please.

*December 24*        The untouchable joy of Christmas.
I didn't know what joy was,
never heard of it . . .
This really is Your night.
Never mind what all happened afterward.
Tonight we celebrate You shared our life with us.

*December 28*        We don't relate to each other
as much
as each one of us relates to God.

*December 31*        I have to touch home base—except there is nothing to touch. I just spent fifty thousand lire on groceries. If I think of the things I have to do today—tonight—tomorrow—you wouldn't believe this carousel has any real people aboard.

Felice, the fruttivendolo (greengrocer) was real. He says he is going to quit work and go to Rio di Janeiro. He is always going somewhere. And the woman at the bar . . . how she keeps her head, arguing with her customers—and keeping her bills straight . . . How these commercianti keep their cool . . . They ought to have a special heaven just for them.

My daughter said to me: "Let Rolando in when he comes." She said so three times in five minutes. "He likes to talk about religion." She would like to be specially nice to me these days, but she is afraid she can't afford it. She is afraid that if she is nice to me, she will betray her friend to whom she wants to be nice too. She can't "divide" herself—as if what she gives me is taken away from her friend. You see how quantitatively we think? Someone at the party was talking about abundance last night and my dear husband distantly agreed, feeling himself threatened by the vacuum of another mind.

Abundance . . . I am going to live as if the next forty-eight hours are going to provide me with an abundance of time—as if all the commotion around me by means of a very special personal transformer translates itself into the slow-motion-touch of ordinary people.

Time, and the passing of time, is a human quality—the obsession with time belongs to the domain of the devil—my other self, a self over-and-beyond, is timeless.

Please, if there is no home base to touch, slow me down to touch the people. Untangle me. Make me stand still.

*January 5*

I am reading Rahner: "Sin—the will not to allow God to be God."

. . .

I know,
I never let You be my Lord.
I have wanted You to leave me alone.
I have preferred to be myself
rather than have "Someone Else" run my life for me.
I have rejected this "second-hand-love."
I am all set to fight You
all the way
just for the privilege to stand on my own two feet.
My God, I have so much not willed You—not allowed You in my life.
However did it happen that now I find You: Lord?

*January 6*

If grace builds on nature, so do temptations. And I don't mean that if it is in my nature to steal I am tempted to steal. No, I mean that if it is in my nature to be honest, I am tempted to be "honest"! Temptations present themselves as good. I must have been told this a thousand times, but in my little mind lingers the thought that I am tempted to do bad. I am not! I am tempted to do good—which turns out to be bad.

Any temptation, banking on my sense of realism, counting on my attempts at integrity, has won me over before I even start thinking. I know that my life doesn't start with God, so . . . I might as well be "honest" about it and live accordingly! I know that whatever aspirations I may have, somewhere—insidiously—ulterior motives obscure my vision. Well . . . I'd rather drop dead than make a mockery of something truly good by following my "feigned" motives! So . . .

My Lord, if You were to truly rule my heart, I should have been able to see the sunrise this morning. I did—with my eyes—but my soul is disturbed—and all my instincts are set to figure out why—and I don't know why. And to-leave-it-be is as difficult as if someone were to tell me not to swim while I am being thrown into the water.

I am going to have to be "unrealistic" and convince myself that no matter what ulterior motives may be breeding in my soul, the one I intend to follow is the one that sets me right with You. And even though I am very, very hesitant to believe that I will do what I intend to do—let's hope that I will.

Do you know what it says here on page 266 in my textbook on spiritual theology?

> Purely human love as such is of no value in the supernatural order!

And not to be accused of quoting out of context, here is the rest:

When we love ourselves or our neighbor for any motive other than the goodness of God, we do not make an act of charity, but an act of natural human love, whether selfish love or benevolent love. Purely human love as such is of no value in the supernatural order.

Where does this leave married love? I am absolutely, positively sure that my husband doesn't love me for "the goodness of God." So . . . ?

*January 7*

It seems I am not the only one questioning the authenticity of a one-sided love relationship—because that is what "detached" love is; it gives without expecting in return. In my class "God in Contemporary Thought" (a subject which is tending toward process theology),
even God,
a caring God,
a loving God,
a vulnerable God,
entering into a personal relationship with man,
evoking a personal response,
is a "becoming" God,
because
a personal relationship
must be
reciprocal,
and a reciprocal, personal relationship
is creative,
with both parties becoming!

Now, I am at this point not interested in considering something as far over my head as process theology, but I am

interested in understanding relationships—love relationships.
And a theology that promises me vulnerable Love stirs my
imagination!

January 8

I am going to get
off
my little hobby horse,
disentangle myself from this pursuit of "Love"
and let relations and relationships take care of themselves.
I am out—of the race.

Even God
is detached
in His love for us.
And how much, how much I love Him for that!
If I had not felt Him stop short,
somewhere at the periphery of my being,
I never ever would have had the freedom
to give the little I did!

I say
that things have changed with me "in spite of myself."
I have complained about "interference."
I have been intrigued by the persuasion,
marveled at the fact
that apparently things could be done for me,
but
if I think again
and look again,
nothing has been put over on me.
Nothing has happened
without my consent,
without my wanting it to happen.

There has always been the point where this Hidden Persuader has become detached—and, now that I think of it, if He did not, I would not, and could not, respond in Love.

This is as far as I want to go—talking about love. It seems that about four o'clock in the morning is my most brilliant time of the day—that is, I am most brilliant when I am half asleep!

The difficulty I have in this long drawn-out question about . . . what . . . ? relating . . . ? has less to do with love than it has to do with hope.

Now this is what I mean by being brilliant! Carrying on a discussion involving a's and b's and c's and d's and after equating and multiplying the lot coming up with the answer "X" . . . some unknown that never entered into the debate in the first place. This is what I mean when I say the answer comes to me on "the silver platter of imagination" and that "my feeling tells me that platter is for me." If I have felt I am skirting the truth, I no longer feel so when I hit upon the concept of Hope.

It is time for me to go back. It is time for me to accept that in my depths I am involved in duplicity, that I deceive myself in my "best and most serious intentions," that nothing I "say or feel about love, whether human or divine, can safely be believed," until my love is purged at least of its basest and most unreasonable fears. (This is all Merton.) I have to "receive this God's Love in all simplicity" and the sincerity of my love for others will take care of itself.

As much as I feel incapable—incapacitated—that much room there must be in my heart for hope—and for trust. A trust I don't have—and a hope I don't feel—but if I pray for it at least I feel I am praying for the right thing.

I have been sent on my way so many times being told to be vulnerable—to stick out my neck—and I have been wondering why in the world I should do such a thing and how in the world I can do such a thing . . . and the more I think about it and the more I tell myself Yes-I-would-if-only-I-could, the more incapable I feel myself to be . . . so much so, and so disastrously so that one of these days I am going to be thoroughly convinced that I-cannot!

I would rather not have to be desperate before I learn to see—to trust—to place my hope where it should be. I would rather not learn the hard way. I would rather not—put down on paper—the thought that came to mind just now—that I would pay the price of despair if that would turn me . . . No, I am not asking for trouble. Just, please, give me the stamina to deal with the small desperations of life, the little things that send me down.

If somewhere in this treasured and respected autonomy of my soul I only had enough sense to make at least the beginning of a choice—a choice for You to fill the gap.

*January 9*

If I were to write,
just for my own enjoyment,
what would I be writing about?

*January 10*

I don't want to throw out what I understand process thinkers to be saying, that change, like all perfections, should be applied to God—just because of all the disturbing questions it raises in my mind—one of them being, "If God can change, couldn't He change for the worse?" I want to follow through on my belief that questions that haunt us have a raison d'être. They come about because we are so fragmentary discerning the truth.

So—I don't like the idea of a changing God. But what David Tracy says of authentic Christians is true for me. I live and pray and speak as if God were really affected by (my) action. I live as if God really were Love, struggling, suffering and achieving with man. In fact, in my heart, I do not accept the idea of God being unchanging and self-subsistent. I like what Rahner says some other place, that God's dialogue with the world is a dialogue of paradoxical utterances. The most reassuring experience of this past year has been that apparently paradoxes in religion are the normal fare. So if God "is" and is "becoming," all in the same breath, and if that bothers me intellectually, my reaction is not what it might have been—something like: "It cannot be true," but rather "I don't see."

Regarding God's changing for the worse . . . maybe, in view of this, Christ's having "conquered death" takes on an entirely new urgency?

*January 12*     Apart from everything else He is also a most gracious God. He almost makes me feel like a lady, allowing me the possibility to bow out of the race (Jan. 8) before He lowers the boom.

If I had been able to anticipate the events, I couldn't have made a more appropriate move—and so, whether I want to or not, all hope is invested in You. No more "competition."

*January 13*     How liberating are Your ways—and how much we wear ourselves out going our own!

*January 14*

This is one of those days I want to write, without having anything to write about. My head is full of nothing: irrelevancies or the kind of problematic that I am too close to, to deal with. I would like to stand still—if I could—but I don't even have any desire to approach the spiritual. If it is there, it is not meaningless—or undesirable; it is rather like the negative of a colored photograph, and looking at it my mind is just beyond the point where it can deal with the fact that red is green, and green is red. I don't see. I have no idea what this picture would look like if I could develop it. Nor am I interested—or disinterested for that matter. I could lament the void in me, or around me—if I felt empty—but I don't really. I could, I suppose, for the next half hour talk in paradoxes, pretending I am sitting on a see-saw, in the middle, unbothered by the unbalance, but . . .

It looks as though I am neither here, nor there, nor very much inspired. I am going to make the beds and do some ironing.

*January 16*

"Being" is not really some static immobility. At least it isn't so in physics. I seem to have a picture in my mind of some frantic microscopic activity in an object that by all appearances is as static as static can be. How much in the physical world is kept into being merely by tension, by the continuous interplay and interaction between one substance and another. Remember, we would be hurled off this globe and into space were it not for the force of gravity. Yet, at the delicate point of balance between these two powers, we feel quite secure—even blissfully unaware! Action is reaction? How much more intricate must be the intellectual and spiritual forces that hold into being—a person.

*January 18*  I find myself "backing up." I am creating a protective distance. Becoming aware of this instinctive move, I realize the significance of yesterday's neither-here-nor-there state of mind. If we function at different levels, then it is my psyche that has a hard time keeping up—I am psychologically tired. Why? He-calls-me-friend and he may be leaving . . . "for a while," he said . . . and this upsets me.

To my amazement my reaction has been quite contrary to how one would expect a person to behave who claims to be incapable of non-possessive love, (and I said I'd never mention the word again!) because I am sincerely happy for him to go, pleased to have him interested in a project he feels is worthwhile and unconcerned about the fact that his absence will leave me without the help and the friendship I need. All this, mind you, without me telling myself to be charitable. All this is actually me. But I am not used to myself functioning with this kind of intensity. I am tired.

Some education I am getting! Because the "backing-up" truly leaves my spirit and my will in His hands.

*January 20*  More than anything else I need to be cured. No matter how noble my intentions are, I am handicapped in the most literal sense of the word. "Your faith has cured you." You have said so, so many times. The problem is, my sophisticated mind doesn't expect miracles—I mean instantaneous turn-of-the-hand miracles. I do expect, though, the miracle of being made-over . . . in time . . . I much expect that, because, Lord, if You don't, how am I ever going to move?

*For love is strong as Death,*
*jealousy relentless as Sheol.*
                    *Song of Songs 8:6*

*January 26, 1981*    Thus I read
                      John's "Farewell discourse":
                      "It is for your own good
                      that I am going . . . " (Jn 16:7).


*January*             "A time for sadness
                      is a time to understand"
                      . . .
                      from the record
                      "Breakfast in America."


*February 3*          I like that: "You see how the crowd is pressing around you,
                      and yet you say, 'Who touched me?" (Mk 5:31). I just love
                      those slightly cynical, down to earth remarks, like: "Lord, we
                      do not know where you are going, so how can we know the
                      way?" (Jn 14:5). Sometimes I would have liked to see the looks
                      on their faces.


*February 4*          Our wedding anniversary:
                      Just give me the name
                      of one
                      married
                      saint!


*February 4*          Merton: The freedom of God's gift of Love, life, calls for the
                      response of our own freedom: a consent to exist in
                      dependence upon his gift.

Then let me understand that I do not consent in
order to exist, but I exist in order to consent.

And all this in an age of much heralded independence and
autonomy! The gift of obedience, a gift of love which consents
in all things.

February 6

Charity is a love for God which respects the need
that other men have for Him. Therefore, charity
alone can give us the power and the delicacy to love
others without defiling their loneliness which is their
need and their salvation. (Thomas Merton, *No Man
Is an Island*).

I asked You: Is it wrong for me to want to enter into the
other's life? And the answer is: Yes, it is wrong.

If I love a person, I will love that which most makes
him a person: the secrecy, the hiddenness, the
solitude of his own individual being, which God
alone can penetrate and understand. (Thomas
Merton, *No Man Is an Island*).

February 14

Lord
I examine myself before You.
I see
what is great and what is small.
What is of interest to me?
Are my worries,
my fears
and my expectations

important?
What is essential?
What can I do without?
What is fruitful?
What is sterile?
What is true?
What is camouflage?
Much is obviously
of so little significance
that I may as well forget it,
though
it was important to me.
Much appears
of such weight
that I should be prepared
to change many things
to conquer it.

More important
than my achievements
is my faith.
More important is that I do
what You want to do in me,
so that I will come to be
the one
I am
in Your mind
and will.
Amen.
(Paraphrase of a prayer by Thomas Merton.)

*February 20*

I haven't written about myself for such a long time, it seems. Mostly because I much need to leave matters in Your hands. Among other things,
many
other things,
what I need to leave with You
is not my love,
but my hang-up.

*February 23*

I have prayed so many times to take away whatever couldn't meet Your eye and You have done so much almost painlessly to me. The question if I would be willing to rid myself at any price is, in all honesty, an open question. I am like Peter, intending to avoid the cost, and You rebuked him and said:

> Get behind me, Satan! You are an obstacle in my path, because the way you think is not God's way but man's (Mt 16:23).

*February 24*

The dignity of our humanity! How much and how often have I considered my humanness a drag or a threat to my spiritual aspirations! And how much am I inclined to propose to myself the impossible choice of either–or: either I operate on a human level, or I mind the matters of my soul. I continually incite half of me at war against the other. And then I turn around and ask You for a favor—the favor to be able to "externalize" once in a while. But I can't, can I, if I believe in this dichotomy of body and soul!

This either–or choice I give myself is the choice of the non-believer. If our Christian faith tells us that Christ has "dignified our humanity" by becoming man, He has given us a chance to pull the two together. Another one of those truths that I have been told so many times and that has never touched my soul.

February 25

It seems that the only relevancies in religious life are "I cannot" and "I do not know," and do nothing—remembering the flowers in the field that "never have to work or spin" (Mt 6:28). Nor does the pine tree here in front of my window! It is so still that each of its needles has caught one glistening drop of rain. Too bad I am not a poet. But maybe it is enough to see, and pray to stand still. Or is it?

I swear, every glorious piece of truth that reveals itself to me seems to be self-destructive and self-defeating and above all unspeakable. If I could just keep my hands off my soul and my prayers and whatever else in me that is trying to pick up the right wave length, something might just come about.

February 26

Maybe I can't approach others because I haven't ever approached their particular kind of suffering?

Other people's sickness and depression make me angry. At the very best I feel "sorry"—and a sorry feeling that is! However, my own suffering opens a door to compassion within me. God knows I am not asking for suffering, but every time I give it a wide berth, I am depriving myself—and the other. That is the theory of it.

Without going into details on the subject, this is a new thing to me. All I can think of is the religious phrase "the redeeming power of suffering." Very distracting big words, but I can't afford to lose if only a glimmer of that kind of truth.

I am writing this down, just so I have something to read
the next time the bomb hits me.

In the dialect of the "Achterhoek," in the east of Holland,
there exists no word for love.
My father is from the Achterhoek.

Tomorrow is Lent.

O my God,
relying on thy infinite goodness and promises
I hope to obtain
the pardon of my sins,
the help of thy grace
and life everlasting
through the merits of Jesus Christ,
my Lord and Redeemer.

If I give up
just let me give up.
I should have done that a long time ago anyway.
But, please,
don't let me rebel.

Good way to start Lent!
For the telling tale is, that I, miraculously,
have also gained two kilo.

*March 4*   The Joy of Ash Wednesday:
"Remember, unto dust you shall return,"
and all your aches and pains
will turn out to have been nothing.
Are nothing!

*March 8*   It isn't enough to have given away my sins to Christ on the
cross, I have to find my life there! Does that mean I have to
leave it there?

*March 9*   I haven't thanked You for anything
for a long time.
Thank You.
Especially for the Good
that I don't really appreciate right now.

*March 10*   I am not "involved." I am involved with what he stands for.
But what does he stand for? For the experience of God in my
life? Or for everything however good and beautiful that
confirms my ego?

   The truth will set you free, it has been said. Right now I
haven't got the spiritual or the physical strength to extend
myself into this freedom. I am tired. I have a suspicion,
though, that the truth by itself—that is, our mere
acknowledging the truth—does not set us free! There remains
the tedious painful process of subjecting ourselves to it.

   What did the liturgy say this first Friday in Lent? It is not
the demonstrative fasting, but the practice of charity and
justice in our lives that will heal our wounds (Is 58). And my

wounds are many. The wounds of illusions. My highfalutin' illusions. But then, there is always Lent—and the continuous prayer that our observance of Lent and the discipline and the fasting and the abstinence and all the rest of this unpopular litany may transform our lives.

*March 12*

Day of Recollection:
Jesus went into the desert—alone.

*March 17*

What does it matter
exactly what I am tied up with?
I am tied up hands and feet
and it is no use
hoping,
wishing,
praying
I would be free,
because there is too much of me that doesn't want to.
Much like the prayer "Help my unbelief" (Mk 9:24)
there must be one "Help my not wanting to,"
but even that is double talk.
I do not want to!
The very best I can do is play dumb and be quiet
and hope to let You be.

From today's liturgy:

I am not finding fault with your sacrifices,
those holocausts constantly before me;
I do not claim one extra bull from your homes,
nor one extra goat from your pens.

What business have you reciting my statutes,
standing there mouthing my covenant,
since you detest my discipline
and thrust my words behind you?

You do this, and expect me to say nothing?
Do you really think I am like you?
You are leaving God out of account; take care!
Or I will tear you to pieces
where no one can rescue you!
Whoever makes thanksgiving his sacrifice honors me;
to the upright man I will show how God can save
(Ps 50).

Yes, I can see I have been pestering You with my "sacrifices."
I recite Your statutes
and profess Your covenant with my mouth,
and, yes, I detest the discipline
and
I don't
offer praise as a sacrifice . . .

Three times I read this psalm today, and not until the
third time did it finally hit me. I am-so-blind. And then, when
I opened the book of psalms in search for a song of praise, I
opened up to Psalm 145: Hymn of Praise to Yahweh the King.
I wouldn't believe anyone telling me of such a coincidence!

*March 20*

If I experience my penance as penance, it only goes to show
how very far removed I am from God's will which is Love and
which should delight me?

*March 25*       Feast of the Annunciation:

     Already it began with Naaman whose desire to be cured had to be translated into the stupidity of bathing seven times in the Jordan (2 Kgs 5). The vulgarity of it all! "If the prophet had asked you to do something difficult, would you not have done it?" his servants urged him. Something difficult, or something "spiritual" or "religious"?

     And here it is again! Today, right in the middle of my rather fanatic attempt to keep alive the spiritual life in me (whatever I dream that to be, all it does is make me cry), right at the point where I am beginning to seriously wonder whether I am cut out for that kind of a life, today we celebrate that the Word becomes ordinary flesh!

> You who wanted no sacrifice or oblation
> prepared a body for me (Heb 10:5).

Christ "materialized" his spiritual life. And that is exactly what I am trying to avoid! Supposedly because I don't see the connection between spirit and flesh. Muchly because I don't like formalism or discipline. It is the spirit that counts, isn't it? But mostly because I prefer to please myself. Behind all the ambitious talk of spiritual living lies the sure comfort of escape. The escape of the drag I am to myself. I have got myself tied up to this and tied up to that, hands and feet, and I much prefer to suffer myself that way, rather than to untie the knots. Believe it or not, just the thought of moving away from my hang-ups repulses me.

     I have to get down to the nitty-gritty translation of my belief. Some of this jealously protected inner life has got to "become flesh." So . . . I'll do the laundry and vacuum and iron and shop and keep house, praying that the Lord will attend to the economy of my soul.

*March 27*    I bought myself a plant.
A blue, blue, blue, electric blue flowering plant.
It is very comforting to look at
because
it doesn't attempt to be anything
other
than blue.


*March 27*    I — can — not — go — back!

It is Jeremiah who keeps whispering in my ear.
Something I have freely translated as:
Keep listening
and keep walking,
especially keep walking,
and — don't — look — back!
The text:

>    Listen to my voice,                        /
>    then I will be your God
>    and you shall be my people.
>    Follow right to the end
>    the way that I mark out for you,
>    and you will prosper (Jer 7:23).

It is like walking on one of those moving sidewalks, going
against the direction!

*March 29*

I talked with a neighbor. She is a saintly woman and always talks about religion, or counts her beads. She is Islamic. We touched on suffering and what to pray for in times of suffering, but we didn't speak the same language . . .

*March 31*

He brought me . . . to the entrance of the temple,
where a stream came out . . . and flowed eastward . . .
He then made me wade across the stream;
the water reached my ankles.
He measured off another thousand
and made me wade across the stream again;
the water reached my knees.

He measured off another thousand
and made me wade across again;
the water reached my waist.
He measured off another thousand;
it was now a river which I could not cross;
the stream had swollen and was now deep water,
a river impossible to cross.
He then said, "Do you see, son of man?" (Ez 47:1–12).

All I see is that this life giving water can drown us! There is nothing in me at all that is either poetically or piously entranced by this Ezekiel's river, with the water rising every thousand cubits, from my ankles, to my knees, to my waist, to the point where it was "impossible to cross." Of course, it wasn't impossible. It was only impossible to cross—and live! I can just about hear the water ringing in my ears.

He took me further (!)
then brought me back to the bank of the river.
When I got back,

there were many trees on each bank of the river.
He said,
. . . wherever the water goes it brings health . . .
Along the river, on either bank,
will grow every kind of fruit tree
with leaves that never wither
and fruit that never fails . . .

✳

Pause a while and know that I am God . . . (Ps
    46:10)

I may never again in my life be given the possibility to
"choose" to do the will of God. Merely "doing" His will is
more often than not an acceptance of the facts of life, a
submission to a "fait accompli" which would be accomplished
anyway, with or without our consent. "Choosing" to do His
will is another matter. It implies I have an option. It also
implies I know His will.

I don't "know" His will. I only choose to leave things be
as if they were His will. The option is that I can interfere! This
choice is creating havoc in my soul. I am sure in the whole Old
Testament no holocaust has been offered equal to mine. And
He doesn't want holocausts! If it had not crossed my mind
that this may be my one and only chance, I would have
avoided the issue. As it is, I am facing it, but God knows how
ungenerously and how ungraciously.

Yes, there is a core of me that would worship and would
love and would "know Him to be God," but there is also the
recognition of the state of affairs in my soul. The plain truth is
that I would not bother "choosing" if there really were an
easier alternative way out.

"Pause a while," You said, "and know that I am God."
All right, this is more than a stalling for time. It is a pause.

And in that pause, yes, everything I have needs to and wants to acknowledge that You are God.

※

My blue plant collapsed, subdued by a hot sirocco which evaporated fifteen centimeters worth of water in a big basin full, outside. It collapsed and revived—and in the process took in as much as three liters of water! Looking at the petals and the leaves I wonder just where those three liters are?

※

I have been trying to understand why, all of a sudden, I am having such a headache trying to do the right thing. It is because so far I have been doing all the right things as a matter of course; and those that didn't suit me I didn't even consider twice. By doing-the-right-thing I mean the ordinary but expected sacrifices we all make as parents or as wives or as friends. So who thinks twice about that? If you don't live up to those expectations you feel like a louse anyway.

*April 5*

As for our salvation, the only thing that is relevant is not our intricate psychological reasoning, not how we are conditioned, not our complicated motives, but our guilt. By the time Good Friday comes around, the only thing that matters is that we are guilty—and have been forgiven.

| | |
|---|---|
| *April 7* | The Bible doesn't say:<br>"The truth will set you free";<br>it says:<br>"If you make my word your home . . .<br>you will learn the truth<br>and the truth will make you free" (Jn 8:31–32). |
| *April 8* | I do not accept myself as I am.<br>Much of my religious endeavor is based on that fact.<br>The promise of a better life,<br>the grace,<br>the sacraments,<br>all serve in my endeavor to be different,<br>because I can't stand myself<br>hung-up. |
| *April 9* | Life would be a lot simpler<br>if I stopped asking the question "Why?"<br>The one answer I get is even more devastating than the other.<br>And they are all wrong!<br><br>Why do I feel rotten?<br>Eliminate the "why"<br>and I just feel rotten,<br>which is bad enough<br>but manageable. |

*

If white blossom trees look like brides,
the little tree down the street
looks like it eloped.
It's too young to be married.

*April 10*

It seems that God is no longer close
and familiar
and friendly.

*April 13*

This is from a book on women in the Bible:

> The sacred record of woman's special creation (Gen
> 1:26–27; 2:18–24) declares not only her full
> humanity but also her superiority to the lower animal
> world which God also brought into being.

My dearly beloved husband says that does not guarantee a
woman's superiority to the higher animals!

❋

"If it doesn't hurt, it isn't love," says Mother Teresa of
Calcutta.
It looks as though I finally see the truth of that.

*April 15*    Jesus did not accept anything-and-everything as "the Will of the Father." He prayed and picked His time. How many times did He walk away from a crowd that wanted to stone Him?

✳

Love is a decision, they say. Maybe the trouble is that this seems to me so totally against a woman's nature. Unless I feel that I have my heart in it, it isn't real to me.

*April 28*    I can't bypass Easter without mentioning it,
but what is there to mention
other than that it seems to have been
the first Easter of my life.

✳

The luminous thought came to me that I prefer the suffering to the void—or to my own complacency for that matter. It is easier to turn to God from suffering than it is from self-sufficiency, complacency, mediocrity or any form of idolatry . . . I thought. Why? Because we can submit to suffering . . . I thought. But why shouldn't I be able to accept everything else—mediocre—and turn?

*May 5*    God,
"my agent."
Just writing it
to remind myself
makes me cringe.

I don't need to go against myself
as much
as I need to follow You.


*May 7*        Talking about today's tendency toward materialism, affluence
and alienation, someone said yesterday: "Man today has
everything. He owns a house. He drives a car. He has a wife."
And in that order too! No comment from his audience either.
And they were all dressed to the teeth. Black, and white collar.


*May 10*       If He is the shepherd
and I am the sheep,
my faith in Him
really isn't my doing as much as it is His.


*May 11*       I lay down my life in order to take it up again.
No one takes it from me (Jn 10:17–18).


*May 14*       I am not putting myself through any exercises. Nor offering
any sacrifice. Nor meaning to walk out on an attachment or a
hang-up or whatever, with the objective of gaining my
freedom. Instead I am relinquishing my freedom—the freedom
to do as I please—and I am relinquishing my independence,
because I choose to be dependent and "listening." I mean to
think in terms of His love—His consoling love—and the
response of freely given obedience. Until the end of
September? The question mark is because I have experience

with myself. The idea is, however, that no matter what powerful reasoning I come up with to "reconsider" or "change my mind," I do not have a choice! I am bound to the formula of my decision, which is a token only of the underlying gift of freedom.

*May 14*

For my family to put two and two together
(which is what I want them to do)
they have to have the two:
the evidence in my life
and the reference!

*May 14*

Headline in the Daily News:
Pope Out of Danger After Pistol Attack in St. Peter's Square.

*May 15*

Mehmet Ali Agca has accomplished the impossible. He has triggered off the most impressive ecumenical movement of our times. All the world is praying for the Pope. And the word from Vatican Radio is:

Do not weep for me;
weep rather for yourselves
and for your children (Lk 23:28).

*May 25*

"Whatever faith she had must be lost forever,"
they said.
And they were talking about me.

And these are the ones I sat with
through the whole of this year
and talked with over coffee.

Whatever
or whomever
do
I
talk
about?

*The flash of it is a flash of fire,*
*a flame of Yahweh himself.*
                                *Song of Songs 8:6*

*December 9, 1981*   This page
is for all that is unsaid
and unwritten,
and to remind myself
that in my life,
I hope to remember
it is His word that is relevant.
Not mine.

*December 23*   There are so few people who will admit to their own
inadequacy. And then of those who do, there are fewer still
who keep on going in spite of it!
He does.

*December 28*   I had a dream.
In my dream I had a prisoner,
a woman,
and I was abusing her,
finding I enjoyed the abuse.
I considered the enjoyment
and found its attraction gratifying,
but shallow
and hopelessly terminal.
I collected myself and said to the woman:
"There is nothing I can do about you being a prisoner."
And then:
"Part of us is good and part of us is bad.
Let's forget about the bad and do the good."
When I turned away from her
I found myself in the kitchen of friends,
in their mountain apartment.

Our usual Saturday evening group of friends
was in the living room.
I was cooking on the Abruzzi wood-stove.
I was frying meat—small pieces of meat.
I had the frying pan in one hand
and a pair of fireplace tongs in the other,
and was trying to take the rings off the top of the stove
to get better access to the fire,
because some of the meat had fallen in.
It was burnt beyond hope.

While I was concentrating on retrieving the meat,
I turned around.
A woman was standing in the open doorway
looking in,
facing me.
The night was clear and serene behind her.
She was dressed in white.
She had angelic hair and a beautiful face.
I knew she was my prisoner.
I looked at her hands which had been bound,
but her hands were free,
her arms relaxed to her sides.
I waited for her to turn around
and flee,
but she didn't.
She stayed.

I woke up,
hearing myself say, out loud:
"Too bad in real life it isn't that simple."
And I knew
without any second thoughts
that the woman was me.

| | |
|---|---|
| *January 9* | The dream didn't tell me to forget about my sins, but to accept them as part and parcel of the good I must go out and do. And the Lord help me if I ever do forget they are part and parcel. |

✳

The most treacherous temptation:
to want to set the world right!

| | |
|---|---|
| *January 13* | Jesus did not come to take away the misery of the world, but to confront it. Watch the connotation of the concept "confrontation." His has nothing aggressive about it. It is rooted in the Father and therefore in love, and it can be ours inasmuch as we are grafted onto his "vita." |

| | |
|---|---|
| *January 14* | It takes humility to suffer. |

| | |
|---|---|
| *January 16* | As for "staying with" people, how about this: |

You wish them peace and love,
and if your peace comes back to you . . .
pack up and leave (Mt 10:11–14).

That's a quote—
more or less.
So, no reason to stay if "your peace comes back to you."
That is something anyway.

*January 22*

He went home again, and once more such a crowd collected that they could not even have a meal. When his relatives heard of this, they set out to take charge of him, convinced he was out of his mind (Mk 3:20–21).

I like that! Guess what I actually read the first time around:

His relatives set out to take charge of him and convince him he was out of his mind.

*February 3*

Just read two articles about the Fierce People—the Yanomamo Indians in the tropical jungle of Venezuela—and wondered how He would have managed there! How could He have talked about the Father? Yahweh and His chosen people is a miracle all by itself.

Maybe it wasn't foresight on the part of the Lord to be born when and where it suited Him, but part of the process. I mean, maybe the world doesn't evolve its own sweet way, but His? Another one of those truths that has been taught for centuries but that only just now shimmers into my vision.

*February 12*

For all I know about Christ,
what I do know is the least relevant.

*February 26*

I am reading the Song of Songs.
Our human love:
"a flame of Yahweh Himself" (Song 8:6).

100

*March 8*    I am going to write a book on sex in the Bible, all the way from Adam's fig leaf to the Song of Songs. But then, it isn't really "sex" I am thinking about. So what is it?

*March 18*    We are capable of love.
Not just human love,
but the kind of love that involves Yahweh himself,
the kind of love that is unashamed
and unembarrassed
and that doesn't need to hide
from Yahweh God
among the trees of the garden—as Adam did.
Something must have happened
sometime
after the shame of the Fall.
The Redemption?

*March 26*    I wonder at what point faith merges into love and how much of our lack of faith is rooted in self-love? But if it is and if I am right about myself and my own unbelief is hung up on love of self, then the question I have asked myself "How do I make an act of faith?" is answered correctly by the suggestion: "Go about your normal business—in Christ." Normal business is the only remedy against self-love.

*April 1*

I want to "understand" Christ,
but even if I could
that is not what I want.
I am asking to be "touched" by that knowledge.
Yet all I hear is the refrain:

> I charge you,
> daughters of Jerusalem,
> by the gazelles, by the hinds of the field,
> not to stir my love nor rouse it,
> until it please to awake (Song 2:7; 3:5; 8:4).

Why not?
Because "we must be content to hope"?
Because "our salvation is not in sight"?
Because "it is something we must wait for
with patience" (Rom 8:25)?
Maybe we cannot ever "see" Him here on earth,
but we may "have to" when we die?

*April 2*

> . . . even if you refuse to believe in me, at least
> believe in the work I do; then you will know for sure
> that the Father is in me and I am in the Father (Jn
> 10:38).

And what is "the work" You do?
Your "Father's business"?
I am going to change tactics.
I am going to pray to the Son
to help me know the Father.
Maybe that will help me know the Son.

*April 3*　　I wonder if Jesus, speaking about Mary choosing the "better part" (Lk 10:42) and supposedly implying an opposition between the contemplative and the active life, wasn't rather making a distinction between a personal commitment to Him versus the role assigned to us by our social position?

*April 4*　　And suppose I say
Christ did not die because of His message
but because of the way He presented it,
then what?
No compromise and no "tactics!"

And if I have employed all kinds of tactics in my life
to protect myself,
then does that make all un-Christ-like?

*April 5*　　Day of Recollection:
Simply by making us wait,
God increases our desire
and our capacity (Augustine).

*April 6*　　It is the Father who knows about suffering and evil.
Not the Son.
He asked the same question:
"Does it have to be this way?"
Maybe I don't lack faith in the Son, but in the Father?
Please
let me "see" . . .
"in the Spirit."

*April 13*        I have only just found the empty grave,
and no one has told me yet He has risen.

*April 14*        There is no resurrection without death.
·              I am trying to believe in the one circumventing the other,
and it doesn't work.

*April 18*        If there is a resurrection,
there is a resurrection in kind.
Grain produces grain—not daffodils.
And the Spirit will bring forth "fruit that lasts."

We produce our own kind.
And so does the Father:

> I awakened you under the apple tree
> there where your mother conceived you,
> there where she who gave birth to you conceived you.
>
> Set me like a seal on your heart,
> like a seal on your arm.
> For love is strong as Death,
> jealousy relentless as Sheol.
> The flash of it is a flash of fire,
> a flame of Yahweh himself.
> Love no flood can quench,
> no torrents drown (Song 8:5–7).

| | |
|---|---|
| *April 19* | Today I have become your father (Acts 13:34). |
| | I awakened you<br>under the apple tree (Song 8:5). |
| | Under the tree in the Garden of Eden?<br>and our sin<br>served<br>"only to bring about the very thing<br>that You in Your strength and Your wisdom<br>had predetermined should happen" (Acts 4:28)?<br>You became our Father?<br>And we were born<br>"of the Spirit" (Jn 3:7–8)? |
| *April 22* | How do You put up with being present to us? |
| *April 26* | To Ben, who wondered if science would ever answer the question of God:<br>    "No, it won't. If God would ever become within our grasp He would cease to be God. The media proper to the understanding of God is faith. Faith operates in the dark—or, rather, it would be in the dark if it weren't faith." |
| *April 27* | I suppose the best way to get rid of a crowd which is after a free handout is to tell them, "I am the bread." |

*April 29*          Into your hands I commit my spirit (Ps 31:5).

Sad to say
that I do not
entrust
my spirit to You!

＊

 We make a lot of God's "absence" in our prayer, secretly
flattering ourselves with the deception that this is a sign of our
holiness.
 It is not: it is a sign of His transcendance.

*May 11*          Why does hell have to be forever?
          If we "live" in God,
          why should we continue to exist without Him?

*May 16*          If evil were just downright evil, it wouldn't break my heart.
          The sad thing is that it is good: corrupted.

*May 17*          To see the goodness behind the corruption . . .

*May 18*          Unless I go,
          the Advocate will not come to you (Jn 16:7).

          Why not?

*Ascension Day*　　　　　　My Beloved went down to his garden (Song 6:2).

A cloud took Him
and He was lifted up,
taken up into heaven
and He will come back the same way,
and it isn't for us to know
"the times
or the dates
that the Father has decided by His own authority" (Acts 1:7).
Not until "it please to awake"?
(Song 2:7; 3:5; 8:4).

*May 22*　　　　　　My dream has simplified life
but it hasn't made it any easier.

*May 23*　　　　　　Let's say that I am no longer "in Love,"
but then
I wouldn't want to be.

*May 26, 2:30 A.M.*　　Harsh words to say and not entirely true,
but if I were moved only by my dream,
I would be moved only by expediency:
my freedom in exchange for "cooking the dinner."
Where is love?
Or the redeeming power of goodness?
That is what Easter was about, wasn't it?

*May 31*

I suppose
none of this,
neither the depth of my feelings
nor what I believe to be their fulfillment,
is essentially spiritual.
But then,
so what!
Neither am I.

✳

There is only one thing worse than being in tears,
and that is:
not being in tears.

*June 1*

Sometimes talking is such a dead-end-street,
with all the signs facing the wrong direction . . .

*June 10*

"Look not on our sins
but on our faith"
we pray during the Mass.

And I didn't even realize this was my dream all over
again—with a difference!

*June 16*

I will raise up for myself a faithful priest;
he will do what is in my heart and in my mind,
says the Lord (1 Sm 2:35).

*June 17*　　　　　"This is what I pray for," he said to me.

> Out of his infinite glory, may he give you the power
> through his Spirit for your hidden self to grow
> strong, so that Christ may live in your hearts through
> faith, and then, planted in love and built on love, you
> will with all the saints have strength to grasp the
> breadth and the length, the height and the depth;
> until knowing the love of Christ, which is beyond all
> knowledge, you are filled with the utter fullness of
> God (Eph 3:16–19).

The "seduction" of prayer! All I need is to count myself
among the saints and fill-in the spaces between these words
and between these lines with delicious bits of flattery, for
surely this prayer, like all prayer, hopes for and expects its
fulfillment and presupposes a potential . . . and a capacity . . . ?
　　The only thing I truly need to and want to pray for is
humility.

✳

Lord,
the truth,
the whole truth,
and nothing but the truth,
about everything I think I believe in,
is robbed of its essence
because of lack of humility.

*June 27*　　　　　How much goodness we don't accept because of jealousy!

I sleep, but my heart is awake.
I hear my Beloved knocking.
"Open to me, my sister, my love,
my dove, my perfect one,
for my head is covered with dew,
my locks with the drops of night."
—"I have taken off my tunic,
am I to put it on again?
I have washed my feet,
am I to dirty them again?"
My Beloved thrust his hand
through the hole in the door;
I trembled to the core of my being.
Then I rose
to open to my Beloved,
myrrh ran off my hands,
pure myrrh off my fingers,
onto the handle of the bolt.

I opened to my Beloved,
but he had turned his back and gone (Song 5:2–6).

No worldly love survives this kind of non-encounter!
Nor could any other love,
were it not for the tenderness of humility.

"Follow me" (Jn 1:43)
into thin air!

*July 16*    Our pretty daughter is against arms,
against the military,
against Christians—"fanatic-Christians," she says—
against housewives,
against "the average middle class white American,"
against red meat . . .
She's not against smoking
and that doesn't have to make sense, she says.

*July 28*    "The absent God" of Buddhism . . .

I always wondered how Merton, believing what he did, could be interested in Buddhism. I am beginning to understand why, maybe. I can see "Nirvana," the emptiness, the point of no desire. This is where we Christians hope to "find God." But how does Buddhism transcend it—without Him?

✳

Our religious differences only confirm how infinitely far removed from us God is.

*August 1*    Jesus did not feed the crowds regularly, did He?

*August 5*    I have been "remonstrating" (Mt 16:21). In fact, I still am. On principle! Would You tell me to get out of Your sight?

I just do not believe suffering can ever be an "aim." But I wonder. I just wonder about this: "The way you think is not God's way, but man's"?

*August 9*        I don't have to reserve a place in heaven for the rest of the world.
                  He does.


*August 16*       Why is it twice as hard to acknowledge each other's sins, rather than face our own?


*August 17*       This renunciation thing bugs me.
                  So, what is "the right thing" for me to "renounce"?
                  And
                  do
                  I
                  want to
                  "renounce"
                  anything
                  at all
                  in the first place?

                  And I do mean the question mark
                  for each one of the components of the question!


*August 18*       I am beginning to hate myself because I am not "doing" anything. Maybe that is what I am so piously "renouncing": the part of myself I don't like. Where is my dream and the acceptance of everything that is part of me and the turning to the seemingly insignificant good?

                  I am to choose the good,

my own good,
regardless of what's all tied up with it.

Father in heaven,
I didn't think You'd still be around to tell me!

August 29     I don't know which is more of a deterrent to Christianity. A
              dictatorship? Or a general atmosphere of "tolerance"?

                                   ✻

              Regarding the Sunday collection in the little church
              around the corner: the Monday morning Mass will be offered
              for those who leave a gift on Sunday! How about that for an
              incentive.

September 7   If we acknowledge our sins, then God who is
              faithful and just will forgive our sins and
              purify us from everything that is wrong (1 Jn 1:9).

              Maybe this doesn't mean only that I acknowledge my sins
              and you acknowledge yours, but also that I acknowledge
              yours?
              Instead we hand each other an excuse, a way out, a
              chance "to pull ourselves together."

September 9   This inclination to "pacify" is a temptation.
              There is no moral tension—and no breakdown—if there
              isn't at least as much good as there is bad.

Whatever the body spills out, it does so because of a healthy defense mechanism. And so it is with our soul. We erupt with bitterness, because the goodness inside us cannot stomach it all. There is no confession, of any kind, unless we are stirred by goodness.

Pacifying a confession smothers the goodness. The thought makes me sad. We are born pacifiers.


*September 14*    The awesomeness and the reality of the Eucharist!
It makes every other pseudo-religious ceremony
less than child's play.

This morning I took my heartache with me,
and I just sat there
in church,
without any excuses,
without any explanations,
praying to God
He would look at me with kindness
and help me be kind to myself.
And then,
as I said:
the awesomeness and the reality of the Eucharist . . .
and the frivolity
of anything
other than that,
and the sadness,
the terrible sadness.
A sadness, beneficial to the soul.

I have finally stopped thinking that I brought it off beautifully.

*September 27*    Last year, at this time, I was thinking of a way of life which would lead me to being receptive—this year I am thinking in terms of being cooperative; whatever that is supposed to mean?

*September 28*    Come to think of it,
yes,
I would want
someone
to pray to the Father
for my "hidden self to grow strong . . . " (Eph 3:16).

*October 2*    What has happened is that I have filled the emptiness with words and the words are busy-bodies and distort an inner truth which is beyond me. Maybe I would be better off leaving the words out of my prayer.

*October 4*    Don't let me reject
the good things in life.
Doing so never leads me to You.

*October 6*    Just for the record: If a sacrament doesn't lose its power because of the unworthiness of the one who administers it, then I don't see why women can't be priests.
    What brought this on? Today is one of those Masses:

The spirit of the Lord God is upon me, because the Lord has anointed me (Is 61:1–3).

It is what comes after that that interests me. If I ever were to give an honest answer to the question "What would you like to do?" I would spell out Isaiah.

*October 10*

The Lord invited the rich young man to "come and follow me." Period! Something like: "Get yourself organized and come and follow me." That this meant the poor man had to rid himself of a fortune was of secondary importance. If we spend all our spiritual energy on selling all we have and give all our money to the poor . . . and leave it at that, we are treading thin air.

*October 13*

I don't know how such a thing can happen
on an ordinary day like this,
but I found myself praying
with some sobriety
and some presence of mind
to "take my life" . . .
and listening to my own prayer
I wondered if I knew what I was talking about!
But truly,
without very much emotional to-do,
that is my desire.

116

| | |
|---|---|
| *October 14* | If summer has taught me anything, it is to go on. Regardless. Couple that with the statement: "No one who looks back is fit for the Kingdom of God" (Lk 9:62) and you are all set. |

*October 15*    The Justice of the Lord . . .
        And I always thought the Lord was Just because that was one of those things He surely had to be. God is all Good: so He is Just. Part of His perfection. And very awkward in practice if we prefer His mercy.
        I have never reconciled His Mercy with His Justice. I thought God in His Goodness could "afford" our sins.
        He cannot.

*October 17*    Heaven and earth are full of Your Glory,
        but I don't see into this mirror,
        because I am looking at the speck of dust on the glass.

*October 19*    We don't even have to intend to cooperate.
        We only have to allow it to happen.

*October 21*    I feel "off-the-track," through the point of hesitation and derailed. It makes me think of my dream again and my freedom and how I thought it was the turning that had set me free. Not so. It's the fire.

✳

Later:

I have come to bring fire to the earth,
and how I wish it were blazing already (Lk 12:49).

This is today's Gospel!

*October 27*

It is the fire.
His fire.

✳

"Forgiving ourselves" and "giving ourselves an excuse"
are not one and the same thing, as my neighbor says they are.
We need the excuse precisely because we cannot forgive. That
is what is wrong with pacifying. It's not even a surrogate for
forgiveness. It is a decoy.

*October 30*

There is faith
and faith
and faith
and there is a whole lot more faith
where we, Christians, believe there isn't.
"Will only a few be saved?" (Lk 13:23)
What if we, expecting to be first,
turn out to be last? (Lk 20:16)

*November 1*

These are the people who . . . have washed their
robes white again . . . (Rv 7:14).

118

I am wondering.
    The woman in my dream was dressed in white . . .

November 2    Purgatory
for those who cannot, by their own effort,
cleanse their soul.

Who says purgatory is for the dead only?

My dream,
my dream,
and the fire in my dream,
and the totally incomprehensible
and totally convincing vision of the woman who was free . . .

"Purgatory."
I don't like the word.
Maybe it stands up better as an idea,
stripped of its cultural and artistic ballast.

    This is the extent of my writing for a while. None of this
"understanding" touches my soul. He does. In my work. And
I'll pray with all my soul, that I'll, please, let Him.

*Love no flood can quench,*
*no torrents drown.*
*Song of Songs 8:7*

*November 13, 1982*  I am longing for Christmas
and the promise of a new life
totally uncomplicated and simple.

*November 17*  An interior life is not the same as a spiritual life.

*November 21*  Jesus says: "Anyone committed to the truth hears my voice."
How can I be committed to the truth and not allow for
the doubts? On the other hand, how much of my fancy doubt
finds its root in vanity, rather than in a desire for truth? I have
the uneasy feeling that I wouldn't have to be quite as stupid as
I make out, if only I would stop thinking. There must be
something much nearer to "childlike," a purer simple-
mindedness . . . a trust . . .

Lord, why the reluctance to ask You to simplify my life?

*November 24*  Mine is a private religion? Interesting! Now that I find myself
longing for a "simpler" life, wanting to "participate," I find
myself participating in an institutionalized Church!

*November 25*  All right, we are not talking about the "institution" of the
Church. We are talking about "the visible Church," the part
we can see: the "tip" of the iceberg.

Lord, my iceberg is real only under the surface, and there, I am comforted to believe, it includes a lot more than can be seen. My underwater iceberg is so much more real and so much more substantial that the visible tip has become accidental. And I do mean accidental. In fact I was going to say that it could as well have been an island, or a tree, or a cloud, or thin air . . . and then, of course, I am talking nonsense, because "the tip" has got to be the tip of-the-iceberg.

"Why are you a Catholic?" someone asked me, expecting some profound answer.

"Because I was born a Catholic," I said.

"But wouldn't you have become a Catholic?"

"No, most likely not," I answered. "The odds are against such a decision."

"So you just caught it, like the flu," was the angry accusation.

"I didn't just catch it," I thought. "I have made choices. Profound choices . . . all of them underwater . . . "

Looking around me and seeing that the Catholic Church is obviously not relevant to most of the world, I have resigned myself to the evidence and consoled myself with an underwater vision—a "mystical" reality—a reality where salt does function and seed does grow—even though we do not know how. I am enticed by a vision of the world which would proclaim the Glory of God, if only we learned to look past and beyond what is so clearly and disturbingly visible.

So now I am being confronted with a package deal: the whole Iceberg. If I did not have experience with other "package deals" in my life, I wouldn't even consider it. So this is the Church. I wonder what it is like being a Catholic.

＊

I don't like it! I have over-shot the mark. Everything inside me—the underwater-part of me that prays—disowns the choice; or rather, the color I give to the choice. I am being disowned! I am right back at the charming invitation that it all could be so simple, if only . . .

You know, that tip of the iceberg ought to be the simple part!

*December 2*  And I always thought that "building the house on rock" meant that our faith ought to support our actions. Not so. Our actions ought to support our faith!

> But everyone who listens to these words of mine
> and does not act on them
> will be like a stupid man who built his house on sand.
> Rain came down,
> floods rose,
> gales blew and struck that house,
> and it fell;
> and what a fall it had (Mt 7:26–27).

*December 13*     Regarding my "affiliation" with the Church:

I wonder if I haven't disassociated myself for other reasons, and if I haven't built a pearly philosophy of life around a grain of sand: a beautiful cancerous growth. I have been hoarding this thing and now I wonder.

Where in this "package deal" fits in the authority of the Church? And how does it balance with the one and only thing I do believe in, and do stand for: our personal integrity and our personal freedom?

Lord, if I ever have to choose between the two, I'll stand by the privilege and the right to follow my own mind. And if that means I disassociate myself, then so be it. You figure it out.

And that of course is my grain of sand.

And what is my integrity? "Our integrity is like dirty clothes," says Isaiah somewhere. There was a time I gladly relieved myself of this burden in exchange for His word.

Lord, teach us Your ways . . .

I wonder how our dearly-beloved-great-saints felt about the Church?

. . . we are the people He pastures,
the flock that He guides (Ps 95:7).

*December 16*  The difference between the Old and the New Testaments is that the Old speaks of a "relationship" with God and the New is about "life" in Christ. Maybe everybody already knew about that, but I just woke up with that idea this morning at five o'clock. Anyway, my mind is still in the Old Testament, whereas for ages, it seems, the invitation has been to the New . . . to Life.

*December 17*  Not to be self-sufficient . . .
I forget,
Lord,
I forget.

*December 18*  My dream is no longer relevant . . .

*December 20*  . . . because the issue is no longer my freedom.

I suppose
once you know
it is within your power
to lay down your life,
the next step is to lay down your life.

*December 21*  We can "lay down our life."
If we could not,
the grace of God would not be grace.

*December 23*

I never thought of the Church as sinful,
and I am not so sure
this Holy Catholic Church thinks of itself as sinful,
but if it is,
and if it—even sporadically—confesses to be so,
then there would be room for the Lord,
and for grace.

The awesome burden of being entrusted with "The Truth,"
and the righteousness that is claimed because of it!

Lord,
this Church isn't any nearer to You
than anyone of us is.
Nor has it got any ground to stand on
to make any one of its famous claims
any more
than anyone of us has any claim on You.
"Know that I am with you always" (Mt 28:20).
So?
What does this guarantee?
Of all things, it does not guarantee perfection!

Somehow, it seems to me, there is more than a memory of
arrogance about and a whole lot of quack authority. And what
about this all-mighty, all-loving, all-powerful, self-sufficient
God the Church has preached? How much has this concept of
God festered our utter sense of worthlessness and futility?
What do you think it takes for a Church to side with a
powerful God, other than a search for power? How long did it
take us to evolve from God Almighty to a God of Love, a
vulnerable God? Will the Church ever admit to being
vulnerable, other than one, holy, catholic and apostolic?

I think, in fact, it does, but we don't quite believe our ears.

✳

Indignation.
Holy indignation!
My sins have all the wrong names:
self-sufficiency . . .
indignation . . .

✳

Come now, let us talk this over,
says Yahweh.
Though your sins are like scarlet,
they shall be as white as snow;
though they are red as crimson,
they shall be like wool (Is 1:18).


*December 29*    More than I want perfection for myself do I want things to be
perfect around me—which is not a virtue!


*January 6*    I wonder
how much I am adopting his way of life,
which may not be mine!

*January 10*

How I am tempted to tear up all this writing! The only reason I do not do so, I tell myself, is because I like to keep track of the process . . . and remember . . . so that I can help others, I tell myself . . . Lord . . . and if I do tear it up, all this will cease to be real and I'll convince myself nothing like this ever, ever, happened.

As I said before, I do not entrust my spirit to You, but to this paper. And if I would tear it up, would that mean I would entrust my spirit to You? No, I am afraid it would not. With or without the writing I am a long way off.

*January 14*

He calls me friend
because he has made known to me
everything he has learned . . .

And I
have never told him
that, yes, I have accepted
his love.

*January 15*

We have to wait for the right time. If we do, and enter into it, it is like entering into prayer and our actions are infused with something other than us.

✳

I am glad I am already a Catholic. If anyone were to lay down the line, saying that only if I truly "believe" may I receive Communion, I never would—for I don't trust my own faith. The Church kind-of believes "for" me, leaving me an awful lot of leeway.

| | |
|---|---|
| *January 18* | We talked<br>about Love<br>and about accepting love—human love,<br>and about the Trinity:<br><br>"The Son,<br>loved by the Father,<br>accepts this Love."<br>"This is the Love in which we share," he said to me.<br><br>And I:<br>"If that is true,<br>if we are so caught up in creation,<br>and Christ IS,<br>then we can BE!" |
| *January 19* | So Love is not a person-to-person relationship.<br>Nor is it reciprocal.<br>If it were, it would be at a standstill.<br>Nor is it, therefore, "one-sided" and "debilitating."<br>If it were, Christ would not BE.<br>And He IS.<br>All of my soul's eye can see: Christ IS.<br><br>And all my previous arguments about what I thought Love<br>ought to have been like<br>have come to nothing!<br><br>If only I could guarantee myself to remember . . .<br>but I have no words to remember with.<br><br>Nor do I comprehend any more about this "new country"<br>than I would had I just arrived in port. |

I can't even, with any justification, say: "This is a new life,"
for I am sure to have carried all of my old self with me.

I can't truly say:
"I am lost";
"I don't know the beginning
or the end
or the focus of my prayer,"
because I am surrounded by it.

The only prayer that makes sense is the Our Father.
At least I can identify with the Son
and face the Father
and stay put
and allow myself to BE.


*January 21*      Love is not reciprocal,
but outgoing.
Reciprocal love is a concept of the world.


*January 27*      I suspect that my argument against detached love, or
"triangular love," has been based on the fact that it leaves me
unfulfilled rather than incapable of a return, because detached
love, offered, asks for a return of detached love—which leaves
me dissatisfied—because I am interested in and motivated by
the return! Complicated!

| | |
|---|---|
| *February 1* | About the Song of Songs |
| | and about the Love of the Father: |
| | Such is the love that changed the bride, |
| | that comes to us |
| | not because of us, |
| | but because of Him. |
| | |
| | Love |
| | we cannot earn |
| | or deserve. |

✳

Jack Dominian writes:

"The absent or meaningless God can . . . enter our life,
[when and] because we feel loved unconditionally.
We cannot earn or deserve God's love
and, as long as we tried to reach God in this way,
there was an ever receding figure
who could not be reached.
But now God stands still . . . "

| | |
|---|---|
| *February 4* | I find the Church unfolding before me very much like a flower, unfurling each petal right in front of my eyes. But what I begin to see is a sinful Church and the only hope it has is that Christ identifies Himself with sinners. |
| | |
| *February 5* | If conversion implies a turning, I have been traveling the proper speed to make the turn for sometime and now somebody has given me a push in the back. You know what |

happens when that happens? You fly out of orbit. I wonder if I'll fly out in a straight line, or whether I'll continue on some other orbit? I suppose it'll all depend on what is the center of my life.

*February 9*    The Incarnation and the Eucharist . . .

✳

How easy it is to spend spiritual riches—not to mention the fact that we let it slip right through our fingers and squander it. I feel there is just a bare flicker of myself left— and not because I have given all that much!

*February 15*    And the flood lasted for forty days (Gn 7:17).
So that's what Lent is about: Yahweh washes out all evil!
I like this build-up:
the Creation
the Fall
and the Flood—for forty days!

*February 16*    Ash Wednesday and it is snowing in Rome.

✳

Regarding our religious discussions: I think we have to look for a belief we can personally and totally identify with and accept the fact that this will lead to differences, rather than water down our "faith" to a common denominator which is comfortable to everyone. Why? Because faith should lead to a commitment and we will not be moved to commit ourselves, personally, to someone else's faith—much less to a watered-down version.

*February 17*    Christ just spoke the word
and left the revelation to the Father.

*March 4*    . . . too close for comfort.

*March 7*    What does it take for me to pray the way You want me to?

I am afraid that what it takes is . . . ? "An attitude of abandonment," I was going to write, but that too is too close for comfort and has about it a ring of truth which could persuade me—or "set me free," as this conspirator against my Self whispers in my ear.
(This is the time I write most, when I don't want to "listen.")
I would let-go. The trouble is the doubts I conjure up to protect myself: should I let-go? Here we are again in the domain where temptation and inspiration become entwined in my befuddled mind.

All right, here comes "the truth":
—I am disoriented in my prayer, because I must learn a new way to pray.
—I am incapable of this new way, because it involves a change in attitude.

–This attitude has to be changed in my life, not in my prayer.
–If I were to follow my sacred intuition, this change would involve a certain "abandonment" to the present moment . . . and this is where I get lost.

Basically I don't want to abandon myself to the irrelevancies of my life. And I tell myself that—if I do—I'll be right back where I started: without prayer, acting in a vacuum. As far as I know, the temptation seeps in at the point where I tell myself I cannot afford to act . . . blindly. I have to (?) act from a center of prayerfulness—an argument which closes the vicious circle, and—remember—the suggestion (inspiration?) was to get "out" of my prayer, not "back" to it!

March 9

All things in our lives can lead to Christ.

✳

It's about the quality of our lives
and about the Father
and about all glory and honor that is due to Him.

March 10

. . . a quality which is His quality:
the typical Christlike and inexplicable quality
of evil-being-turned-into-good
and death into life.

March 11

Only suffering can break through into the other's life.
That's how He did it.

With a bit of luck
we can get by
participating on the sacramental level.


March 13

"We will not . . . say 'Our God!' to what our own hands have
made" (Hos 14:4).
How much of our image of God
is determined by how we feel about our world
and about ourselves!
Change the set-up of our little egosphere
and God ceases to be.

If we conjure up
some majestic vision of His Glory,
all we need is for one piece of the mosaic to be missing . . .
and He is no more.

It is a miracle we have any notion at all!


March 14

It is a miracle the notion survives!
Not because of our overpowering and destructive attachments,
but because we start with such a poor vision to begin with.
What on earth
do we use
to create the image of our God?

The Golden Calf of our mind!

*March 15*    There is only one thing I am truly interested in talking about
anytime, anywhere, with anyone, and that is man's concept of
and approach to God. If that puts the wrong emphasis in the
wrong place, because it starts with man rather than with God,
then I'll gladly grant that I am starting in the wrong place. I
will grant anybody anything, as long as one articulates anything
at all. The mere search for the inner statement leads to God.

I'll be much more at a loss dealing with the question why
I so desperately need to talk? Am I "called" . . . or
"frustrated," filling the gap of my frustration with words,
only? What makes the question difficult to answer is that I
"feel" frustrated!

What about loneliness and the desire to hear ourselves
talk? How much do we need to hear confirmed our own
beliefs . . . in others? If that is why we talk about God, then
our silence would be better.

*March 16*    I still think that our gifts and our use of these gifts, and even
our responsibility to use them for the good of others, is
secondary only to our first responsibility which is to be
"Good." This includes a life on the sacramental level and
functions as effectively and as unobtrusively as salt.

*March 18*    I am slow.
Just imagine what purgatory is going to be like!
We are reluctant to enter the Promised Land?

*March 25*    Could the fact that the apostles experienced Jesus as alive have
been a mystical experience? If He "stood among them" (Jn

20:19) in the upper room, without bothering with the door,
why did the stone in front of the grave need to be rolled away?
And if it was rolled away, why was it?


*March 28*

To settle for the ordinariness of life
in view of our extraordinary faith
means to settle for the gap in our lives
and for the darkness of our faith
and for a special kind of loneliness.

In the anguish of the Garden of Gethsemane
that is what our Lord did:
settle for His humanity.

If He had not
He-would-not-have-died.


*Palm Sunday*

That's right.
He did more than settle for His humanity.
He settled for "death on a cross" (Phil 2:8).
It wasn't enough to be man.
It had to be that-kind-of-man
subject to the sins of others.

What would it mean for us "not to cover our face" (Is 50:6)?
Can we avoid this crucifixion bid?
It seems to me He did
for a while.

Until one day the time had come.

*Good Friday*　　　We know Christ existed,
and we know He died
but belief in the resurrection of the body is an act of faith.
We only know that His body was never found
and that some experienced Him as alive
and still do . . .

but we move in an eternal Good Friday . . .

unless we believe in an ongoing resurrection,
and reconciliation.